Best Editorial Cartoons of the Year

BRIAN DUFFY
Courtesy Des Moines Register

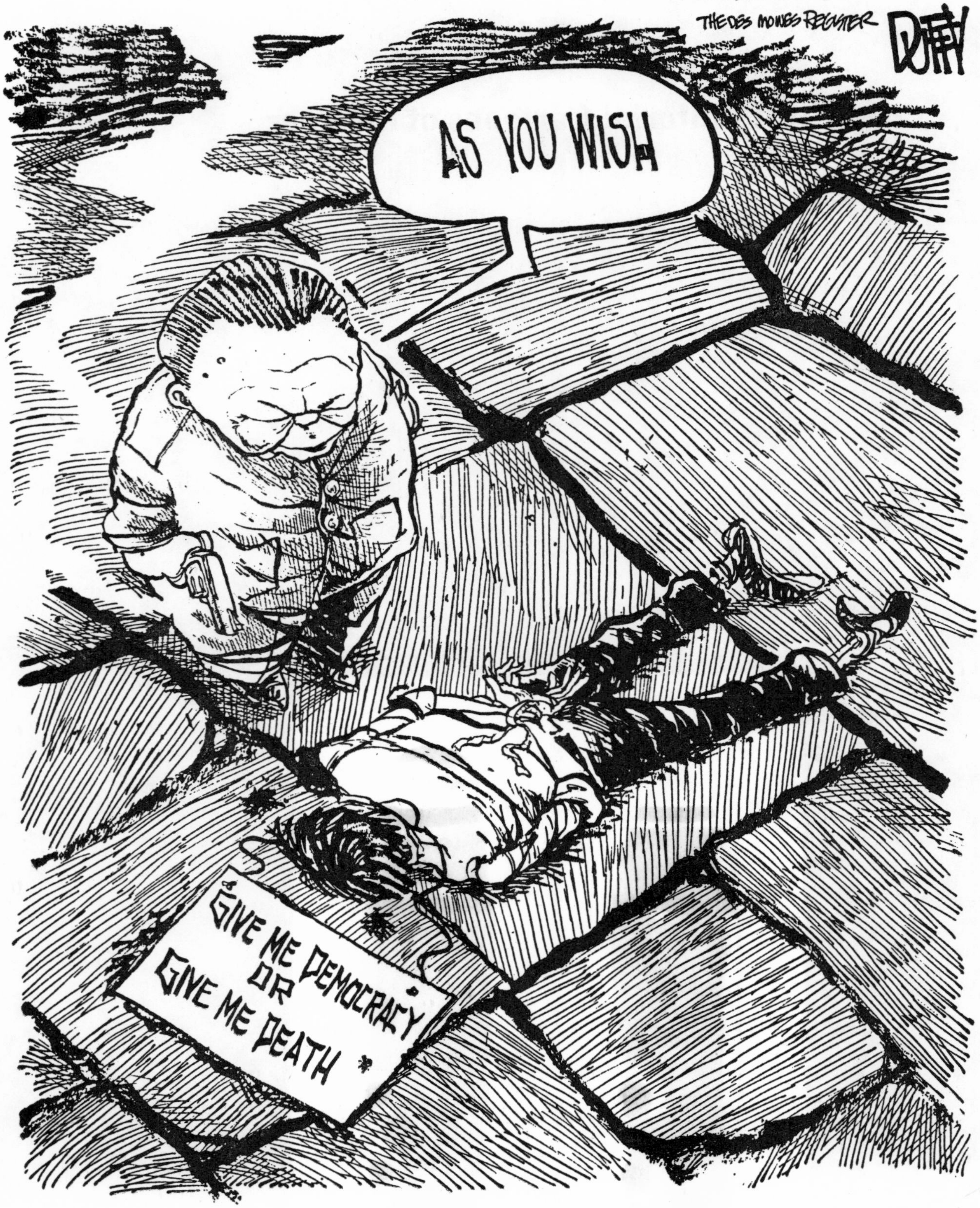
THE DES MOINES REGISTER
DUFFY
AS YOU WISH
GIVE ME DEMOCRACY
OR
GIVE ME DEATH

BEST EDITORIAL CARTOONS OF THE YEAR

1990 EDITION

Edited by
CHARLES BROOKS

PELICAN PUBLISHING COMPANY
GRETNA 1990

The cartoons in this volume are used with the
expressed permission of the individual cartoonists
and their publications or syndicates. Unauthorized
reproduction is strictly prohibited.

Special appreciation to Lisa Diane Hynds Layton for
her inestimable assistance over the past fifteen years
in the preparation of this annual volume.
She is efficiency personified.

Library of Congress Serial Catalog Data

Best editorial cartoons. 1972-
    Gretna [La.] Pelican Pub. Co.
    v. 29 cm. annual-
"A pictorial history of the year."

    1. United States- Politics and government—
1969—Caricatures and Cartoons—Periodicals.
E839.5.B45   320.9'7309240207   73-643645
ISSN 0091-2220   MARC-S

Manufactured in the United States of America
Published by Pelican Publishing Company, Inc.
1101 Monroe Street, Gretna, Louisiana 70053

Contents

Award-Winning Cartoons

1989 PULITZER PRIZE

NEVER CRY FREEDOM IN A CROWDED THEATRE . . .

JACK HIGGINS
Editorial Cartoonist
Chicago Sun-Times

Native of Chicago; graduate of Holy Cross College, Worcester, Mass.; editorial cartoonist for the *Chicago Sun-Times*, 1981 to the present; winner of the 1988 International Salon of Cartoons award, the only American to be so honored; winner of 1988 National Society of Professional Journalists award for cartooning.

1988 NATIONAL SOCIETY OF PROFESSIONAL JOURNALISTS AWARD
(Selected in 1989)

JACK HIGGINS
Editorial Cartoonist
Chicago Sun-Times

VANCE RODEWALT
Editorial Cartoonist
Calgary Herald

Born on a ranch in Alberta; cartoonist for Marvel Comics and *Cracked* magazine; editorial cartoonist for the *Calgary Sun, Calgary Albertan, Calgary Herald*; draws a syndicated comic strip entitled "Chubb and Chauncey"; married to a former Olympic figure skater.

WALT HANDELSMAN
Editorial Cartoonist
New Orleans Times-Picayune

Native of Baltimore; attended Dean Junior College and the University of Cincinnati; editorial cartoonist for the Patuxent Publishing Corporation, 1982 to 1985; editorial cartoonist for the *Scranton Times*, 1985 to 1989; editorial cartoonist for the *New Orleans Times-Picayune*, 1989 to the present; nationally syndicated by Tribune Media Services.

1989 FISCHETTI AWARD

LAMBERT DER
Editorial Cartoonist
Greenville News

Holds two degrees from North Carolina State University; contributing cartoonist for *The Technician*, 1977 to 1978; commercial illustrator, 1978 to 1985; free-lance cartoonist for the *Greensboro News*, 1980 to 1985; contributing cartoonist for the *Raleigh Times*, 1978 to the present; editorial cartoonist for the *Greenville News*, 1985 to the present; cartoonist for two published books.

Best Editorial Cartoons of the Year

JOHN BRANCH
Courtesy San Antonio Express-News

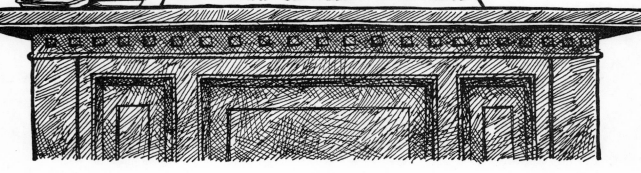

The Bush Administration

George Bush assumed the presidency in 1989, and during most of the year his style was low key. Polls showed, surprisingly, that his approval rating by voters hovered around 70 percent much of the year.

Bush announced his opposition to gun control, but agreed to ban imports of semi-automatic assault rifles. He held firm on abortion and addressed the issue of improving education in the nation's schools. He declared that the Supreme Court was "dead wrong" on its flag-burning ruling and called for a constitutional amendment to prohibit desecration of the flag.

Bush ran into trouble with his nomination of John Tower for secretary of defense, and Congress, after acrimonious debate, rejected the former Texas senator.

The president also launched an offensive against drug trafficking and violent crime early in the year and presented a comprehensive plan calling for sterner handling of drug sellers and users.

Bush and Mikhail Gorbachev of the Soviet Union held a summit meeting off the coast of Malta, but a raging storm kept the two confined to their ships' quarters much of the time. The relatively cordial Malta summit underscored the dramatic improvement in U.S.–Soviet relations over the past few years. The meeting was a tuneup for a more comprehensive summit scheduled for 1990.

ED STEIN
Courtesy Rocky Mountain News

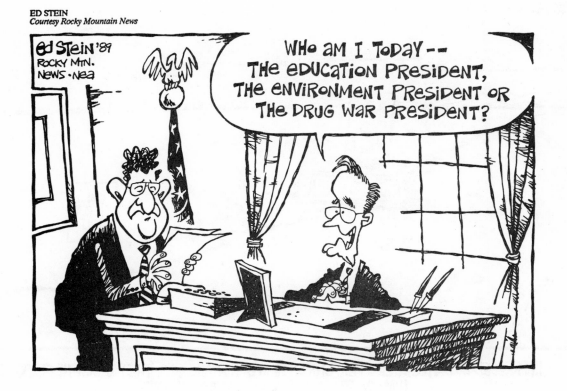

MEET MINDY! SHE'S 14 AND POOR, WITH NONE OF THE "APPLE-PIE" FAMILY-SUPPORT GROUP!

SHE HAS BEEN ABUSED AND RAPED BY HER FATHER! SHE IS PREGNANT!

THIS IS HER 65 YEAR OLD, RICH, WHITE, MALE PRESIDENT—WHO WILL FORCE HER TO HAVE HER FATHER'S BABY!

WELCOME TO GEORGE BUSH'S KINDER, GENTLER NATION, MINDY!

BILL SANDERS
Courtesy Milwaukee Journal

JIM BORGMAN
Courtesy Cincinnati Enquirer

IMPRESSED BY DAN QUAYLE'S PERFORMANCE IN SAN FRANCISCO, THE PRESIDENT STATIONS HIM ON PERMANENT ALERT FOR THE BIG ONE.

JIMMY MARGULIES
Courtesy Houston Post

JOE MAJESKI
Courtesy Sunday Dispatch (Pa.)

MIKE KEEFE
Courtesy Denver Post

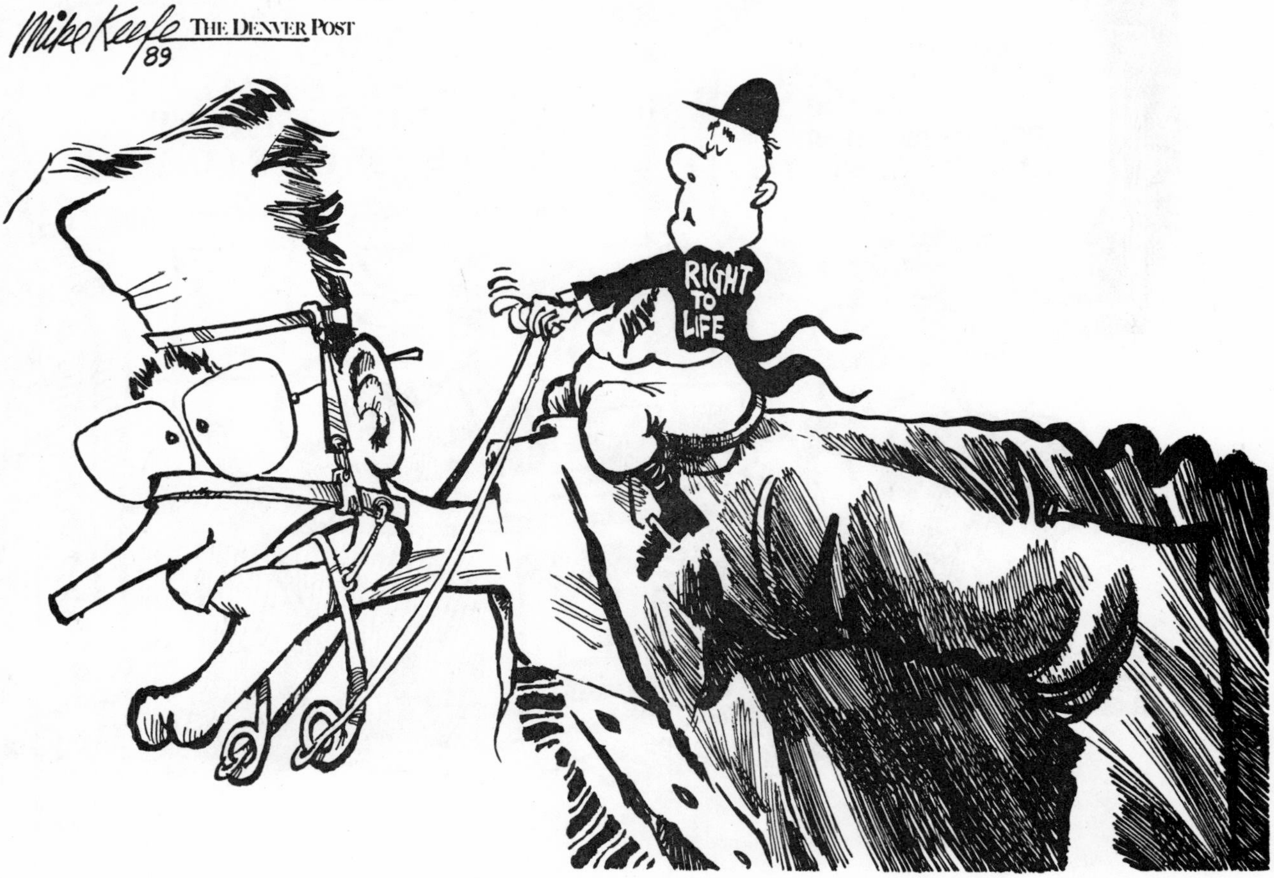
Mike Keefe '89 THE DENVER POST
RIGHT TO LIFE

WALT HANDELSMAN
Courtesy New Orleans Times-Picayune

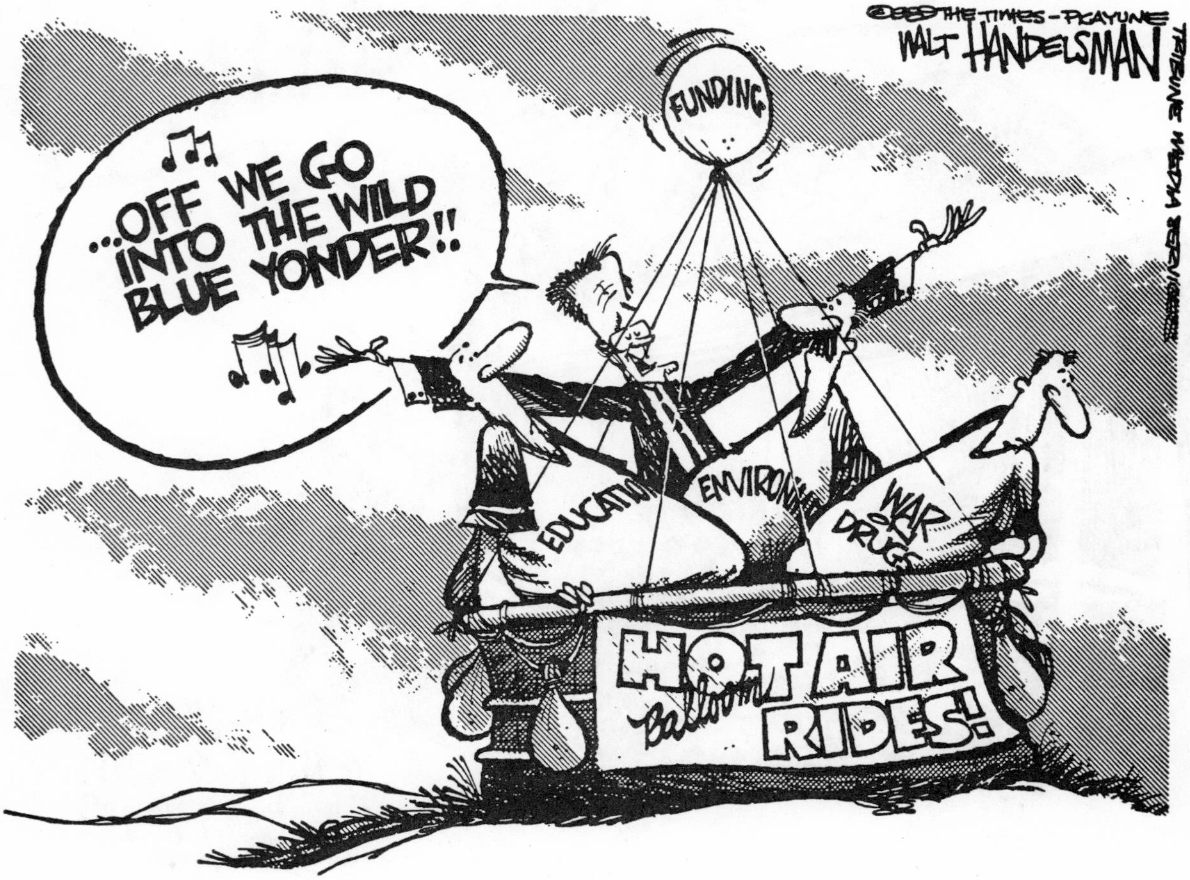
THE TIMES-PICAYUNE
WALT HANDELSMAN
FUNDING
...OFF WE GO INTO THE WILD BLUE YONDER!!
EDUCATIO
ENVIRON
WAR
DRUGS
HOT AIR Balloon RIDES!

"WELL, IT DIDN'T TAKE GEORGE LONG TO GO FUNNY ON US..."

DANA SUMMERS
Courtesy Orlando Sentinel

MIKE SMITH
Courtesy Las Vegas Sun

"THE PRESIDENT IS HERE AND HE WANTS TO SEE THE WEATHERMAN!...NOW!"

HY ROSEN
Courtesy Albany Times-Union

JEFF DANZIGER
Courtesy Christian Science Monitor

DAVID HITCH
Courtesy Worcester Telegram and Gazette

GEORGE FISHER
Courtesy Arkansas Gazette

CHUCK AYERS
Courtesy Akron Beacon-Journal

CHARLES WERNER
Courtesy Indianapolis Star

DRAPER HILL
Courtesy Detroit News

So Long, Ron

Ronald Reagan rode off into the sunset of retirement in 1989, carrying with him the highest approval rating of any departing president since World War II. He left office amid the longest economic expansion in American history. While he was in office, inflation was held in check and 16 million new jobs were created. Supporters declared he also had restored the confidence of most Americans in themselves and the presidency, and that his policy of peace through strength had been vindicated.

Reagan, however, also left some minuses. He passed on to his successor a huge federal budget deficit and a trade gap that was draining needed capital. Furthermore, under his leadership, America had become the world's greatest debtor nation.

Reagan championed the idea of less government rather than more, and sought to withdraw government from areas where he felt it was not needed, or wanted. He also led the fight to lower personal income tax rates. Under his leadership, the top tax rate was reduced from 70 percent to 33 percent.

After leaving the White House, Reagan created a furor when he accepted a $2 million fee for a few public appearances in Japan.

His wife Nancy published her memoirs, entitled *My Turn*, in which she criticized many of the staff who served Reagan while in the White House.

DARKOW
Courtesy San Antonio Light

23

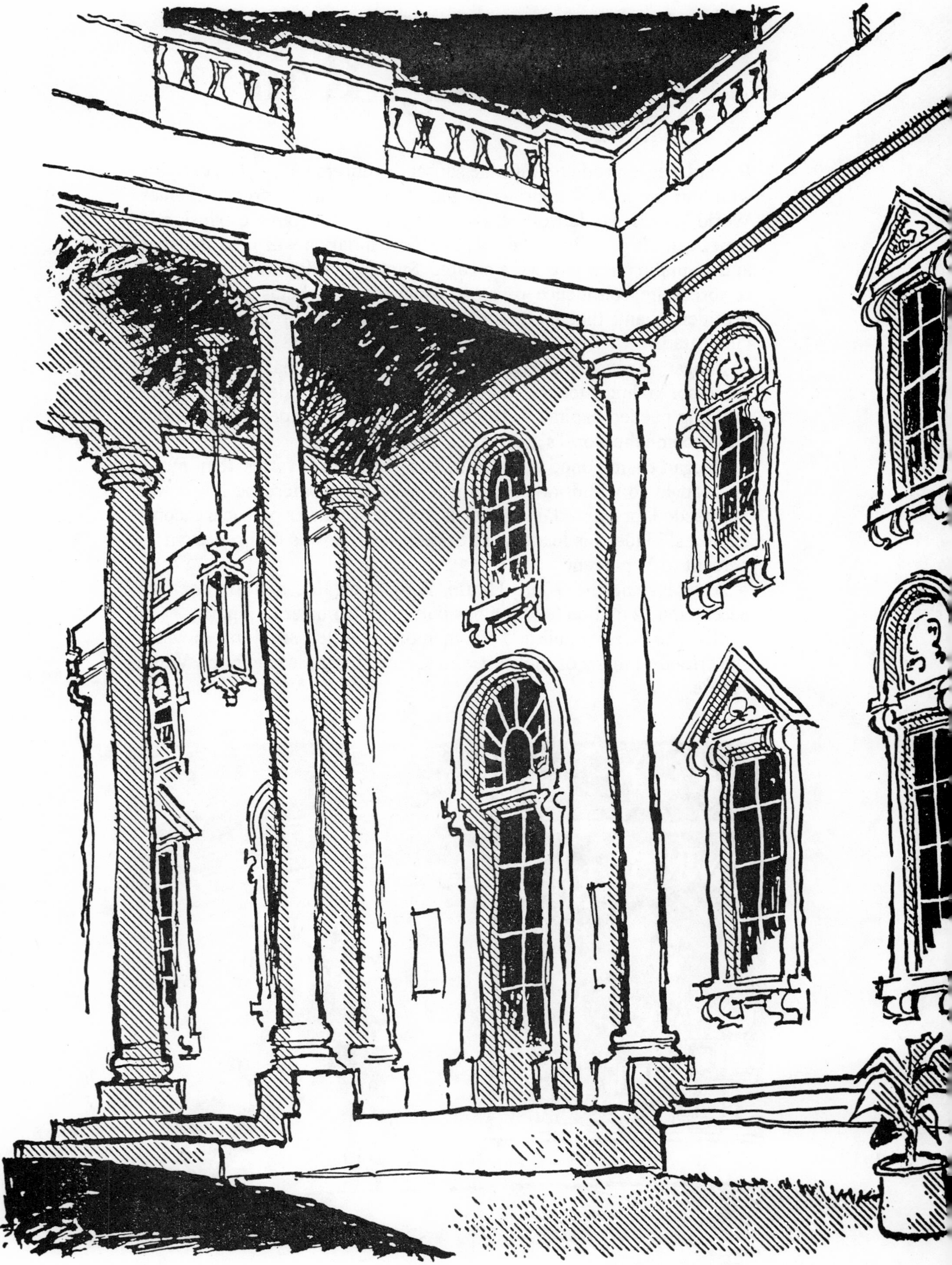

DICK LOCHER
Courtesy Chicago Tribune

TOM ADDISON
Courtesy Associated Features

HE WAS THE ONLY JUROR WE COULD FIND WHO KNEW ABSOLUTELY NOTHING ABOUT THE IRAN-CONTRA AFFAIR.....

MIKE PETERS
Courtesy Dayton Daily News

CLEANING UP GOVERNMENT WASTE AND FRAUD (THE REAGAN YEARS)

ETTA HULME
Courtesy Fort Worth Star-Telegram

STEVE HILL
Courtesy Oklahoma Gazette

CRAIG MACINTOSH
Courtesy Minneapolis Star-Tribune

CLAY BENNETT
Courtesy St. Petersburg Times

' ... Great party, huh, honey?... '

JOHN TREVER
Courtesy Albuquerque Journal

THE SHINING CITY ON THE HILL

Death of Communism?

Mind-boggling changes that few scarcely even dreamed of wracked Eastern European communist countries in 1989, leading many observers to speculate that the world was witnessing the death of communism.

In Poland, East Germany, Rumania, Hungary, Bulgaria, and Czechoslovakia, long-entrenched communist governments were either overthrown or compelled to give up some of their power. A people's revolution had swept across Europe's Soviet bloc countries, and many people were anxious to credit Mikhail Gorbachev and his policy of *perestroika*, or reform.

In Poland, Solidarity, a 10-million-member labor union led by Lech Walesa, won unprecedented concessions from the communist regime and was invited to form the country's first non-communist government since the 1940s. East Germany named a leading reformer as prime minister in an effort to stem the anti-communism tide, but one result was the political demolition of the infamous Berlin Wall that for almost three decades had divided Germany.

Uprisings in Rumania, Hungary, Bulgaria, and Czechoslovakia pushed out communist regimes as the year ended, and the Baltic republics of Estonia, Latvia, and Lithuania threatened to secede from the Soviet Union. If these events did not signal the death rattle of communism, it certainly had been stricken with a grave illness.

MARK CULLUM
Courtesy Birmingham News

TOM ENGELHARDT
Courtesy St. Louis Post-Dispatch

ENGELHARDT
©1989 ST. LOUIS POST-DISPATCH

JACK HIGGINS
Courtesy Chicago Sun-Times

GEORGE FISHER
Courtesy Arkansas Gazette

JOEL PETT
Courtesy Lexington Herald-Leader

ROB ROGERS
Courtesy Pittsburgh Press

JIM BORGMAN
Courtesy Cincinnati Enquirer

BOB GORRELL
Courtesy Richmond News-Leader

DAVID HORSEY
Courtesy Seattle Post-Intelligencer

©1989 SEATTLE POST-INTELLIGENCER
NORTH AMERICA SYNDICATE

MARK CULLUM
Courtesy Birmingham News

ROB ROGERS
Courtesy Pittsburgh Press

©1989 THE PITTSBURGH PRESS
UNITED FEATURE SYNDICATE

BRUCE BEATTIE
Courtesy Daytona Beach News-Journal

GENE BASSET
Courtesy Atlanta Journal

"BELIEVE ME, YOU EUROPEANS HAVE NOTHING TO FEAR FROM A UNIFIED GERMANY."

CHIP BECK
Courtesy Northern Virginia Sun

MARSHALL RAMSEY
Courtesy UT Daily Beacon

SPYDER WEBB
Courtesy Associated Features

Gorbachev faces the Soviet's crack problem...

DINOSAUR STAMPS

STEVE LINDSTROM
Courtesy Duluth News-Tribune

LAZARO FRESQUET
Courtesy El Nuevo Herald

LAMBERT DER
Courtesy Greenville News-Piedmont

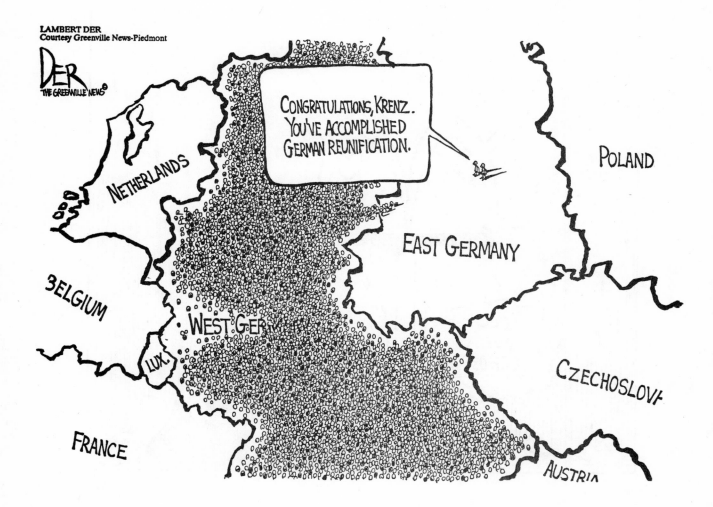

A case where it's not the Rats Leaving the ship!

CHARLES WERNER
Courtesy Indianapolis Star

NEWS ITEM: "FIRST MCDONALDS TO OPEN IN MOSCOW"

JIM LANGE
Courtesy Daily Oklahoman

JACK MCLEOD
Courtesy Army Times

EDD ULUSCHAK
Courtesy Miller Services

JEFF KOTERBA
Courtesy Omaha World-Herald

JACK JURDEN
Courtesy News-Journal Company (Del.)

ART HENRIKSON
Courtesy Des Plaines Daily Herald

CHARLES DANIEL
Courtesy Knoxville Journal

DOUGLAS REGALIA
Courtesy Contra Costa Sun

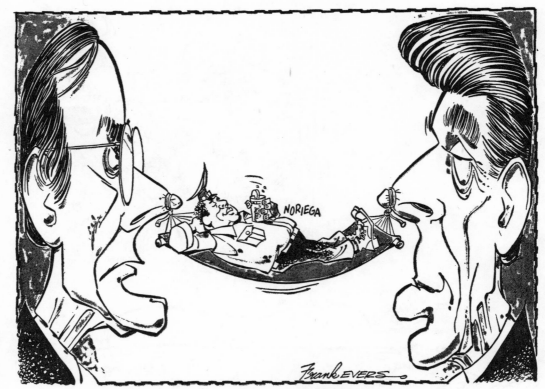

FRANK EVERS
Courtesy New York Post

PAUL SZEP
Courtesy Boston Globe

Central America

Panamanian strongman Gen. Manuel Noriega continued to taunt the United States and President Bush during much of the year. Noriega survived an October coup attempt, but retaliated against his opposition in one of the bloodiest purges in Panamanian history.

In December, Noriega declared that a state of war existed between Panama and the United States. Following the killing of one American serviceman and the harassment of others, the U.S. invaded Panama on December 20. Noriega temporarily escaped capture by seeking refuge in the Vatican embassy. After several days he was persuaded to surrender and was turned over to the U.S. authorities for trial on drug charges.

In embattled El Salvador, businessman Alfredo Cristiani of the right-wing National Republican Alliance won the presidency with 54 percent of the vote. Cristiani moved slowly in keeping his promises to support free-market economics and to negotiate with Salvadoran rebels. Formal talks were held with guerrilla representatives in September, but communications broke down and heavy fighting resumed. Some 70,000 were believed to have been killed in this new rebel offensive that struck directly at large urban centers.

Late in the year, six Jesuit priests were shot to death in San Salvador by uniformed men, and military involvement was widely suspected. Nations around the world pressed President Cristiani for a full investigation.

ED GAMBLE
Courtesy Florida Times-Union

SANDY CAMPBELL
Courtesy The Tennessean

DRAPER HILL
Courtesy Detroit News

MARK FEARING
Courtesy Daily Cardinal (Wisc.)

DAVID HORSEY
Courtesy Seattle Post-Intelligencer

PETER WALLACE
Courtesy Boston Herald

MATT WUERKER
Courtesy Los Angeles Weekly

ETTA HULME
Courtesy Fort Worth Star-Telegram

"IF THE ELECTIONS WERE HELD TODAY, WOULD YOU PREFER TO BE SHOT BY THE CONTRAS OR THE SANDINISTAS?"

China

Unrest grew swiftly in China in 1989 as more and more citizens, particularly students, became aware of better economic and political conditions elsewhere. More than 40,000 Chinese students were studying at colleges in the United States, and thousands before them had returned to China from the U.S. with a knowledge of freedom and a better way of life.

Pro-democracy demonstrations by students began in April, often attracting as many as a million protesters to Tienanmen Square in Beijing. A hunger strike was initiated in May, and protestors later displayed a 30-foot replica of the Statue of Liberty.

The demonstrations grew in size and intensity, and on June 4 a violent government crackdown began. Troops opened fire on the unarmed crowds, killing at least hundreds and wounding thousands.

Chinese leader Deng Xiaoping and his colleagues had decided that massive use of force was essential if they were to maintain control of the communist government. A nationwide disinformation campaign followed, whitewashing the massacre after the bloody streets had been scrubbed. The government campaign to absolve itself generally fell on deaf ears. A disbelieving world remembered the stark drama, shown repeatedly on television, of a lone Chinese youth standing down a column of tanks.

President Bush showed little enthusiasm for imposing strong sanctions in response to the brutal Chinese actions.

FRANK EVERS
Courtesy New York Post

CHINA ATTEMPTS TO IMPROVE ITS IMAGE

JAMES LARRICK
Courtesy Columbus Dispatch

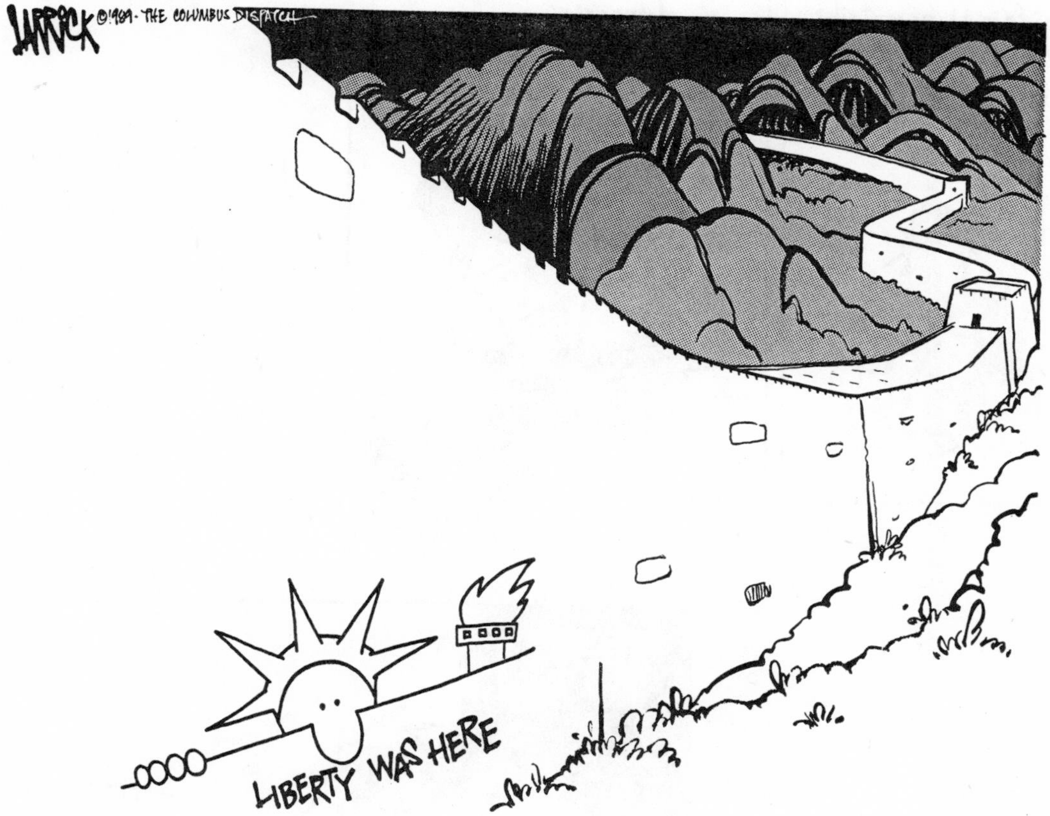
LARRICK ©1989 - THE COLUMBUS DISPATCH
LIBERTY WAS HERE

JOHN DEERING
Courtesy Arkansas Democrat

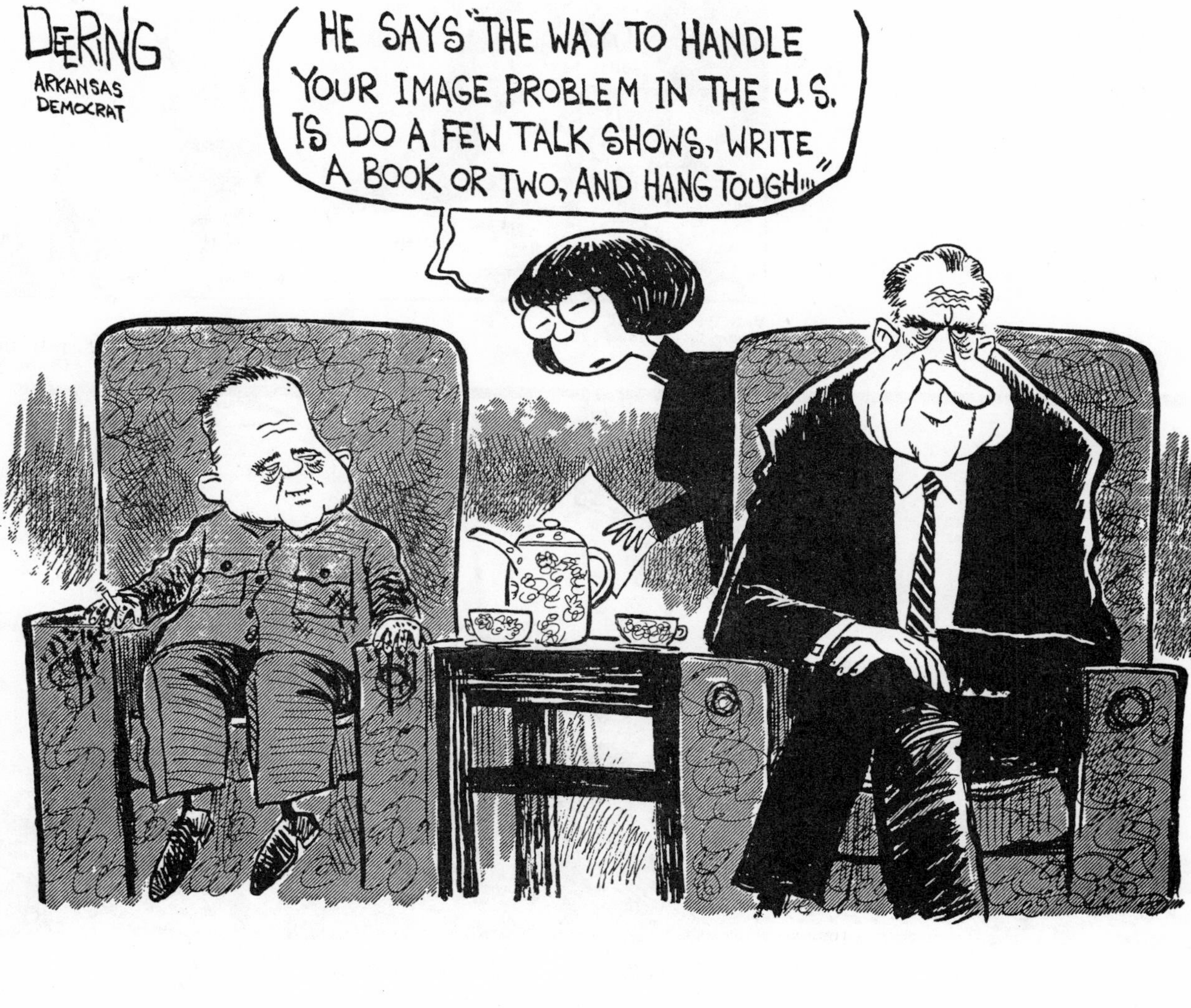
DEERING ARKANSAS DEMOCRAT
HE SAYS "THE WAY TO HANDLE YOUR IMAGE PROBLEM IN THE U.S. IS DO A FEW TALK SHOWS, WRITE A BOOK OR TWO, AND HANG TOUGH!!!"

A Chinese student risking his life in a hunger strike for the right to practice democracy.

An American practicing democracy.

TOM GIBB
Courtesy Altoona Mirror

VANCE RODEWALT
Courtesy Calgary Herald

TOM CURTIS
Courtesy National Review

"Then I asked myself: What would Mao have done?"

EDGAR SOLLER
Courtesy World Reporter

DAVE GRANLUND
Courtesy Middlesex News

MARK CULLUM
Courtesy Birmingham News

KIRK WALTERS
Courtesy Toledo Blade

LINDA BOILEAU
Courtesy Frankfort State Journal

JACK JURDEN
Courtesy News-Journal Company (Del.)

JOEL PETT
Courtesy Lexington Herald-Leader

Apartheid

Sacramento Bee

DENNIS RENAULT
Courtesy Sacramento Bee

Foreign Affairs

British Prime Minister Margaret Thatcher on May 4 celebrated ten years in office. It was the longest uninterrupted term in that office since Lord Liverpool died in 1827 after serving 15 years. Thatcher has been a popular figure at home and abroad, but signs were emerging that support for her policies was eroding. The opposition Labor Party made gains in Parliament, and some of Thatcher's conservative views clearly were not shared by a majority. Her nationalism was seen as unpopular with many voters because of the growing sentiment for European union. Opponents contended she had not done enough to alleviate poverty or to solve environmental problems.

August marked the 20th anniversary of the deployment of British troops in embattled Northern Ireland. The outlawed Irish Republican Army promised to step up attacks on British military personnel and their families to protest the continuing presence of troops. Ten young Royal Marines were killed by a bomb in Deal, Kent, on September 22, and the IRA claimed responsibility.

A new president, Frederik Willem de Klerk, took office in South Africa in September. He promised a five-year reform plan to move his country away from apartheid, but many of the opposition, at home and abroad, were skeptical.

KEVIN KALLAUGHER
Courtesy Baltimore Sun

KEVIN KALLAUGHER
Courtesy Baltimore Sun

JEFF DANZIGER
Courtesy Christian Science Monitor

PAUL SZEP
Courtesy Boston Globe

"LOOK, SEE GORBY GO, . . . SEE GORBY GO ON ARMS CONTROL . . .
SEE GORBY GO ON TROOP REDUCTION, . . . SEE GORBY GO ON POLAND,
ON HUNGARY, ON GERMANY . . . . LOOK, SEE GORBY GO . . . ."

Middle East

Iran's Ayatollah Khomeini informed the world in February that Indian-born author Salman Rushdie and everyone else who took part in the publication of Rushdie's controversial novel, *The Satanic Verses*, were under a sentence of death. The book was regarded as offensive to many muslims. Rushdie, living in England, was forced to go into hiding. Diplomatic efforts to persuade the Ayatollah to change his mind failed, even though the Western world regarded the sentence as barbarous.

After Israeli commandos darted into Lebanon and abducted Shiite muslim cleric Sheikh Karim Obeid, Lebanese terrorists retaliated by murdering U.S. Lt. Col. William Higgins. A new outbreak of violence in strife-torn Lebanon in April left hundreds dead and thousands wounded, mostly civilians.

An Arab League summit meeting was held in Morocco in May. Palestine Liberation Organization leader Yasir Arafat sought to obtain Arab backing for his plan to establish a Palestinian state under United Nations guidance on the West Bank and in the Gaza Strip.

U.S. Secretary of State James Baker called upon Israel to abandon plans to annex the West Bank and Gaza, to halt all Jewish settlement there, and to agree to negotiate a possible withdrawal. Baker also called upon the Palestinians to amend the PLO charter which advocates the destruction of Israel.

JACK HIGGINS
Courtesy Chicago Sun-Times

DON LANDGREN, JR.
Courtesy The Landmark (Mass.)

Berry's World

JIM BERRY
Courtesy NEA

THE HARDEST PART OF A BOOK PROMOTION TOUR? I'D SAY IT WAS DEALING WITH CRITICS.

LARRY WRIGHT
Courtesy Detroit News

BLAINE
Courtesy The Spectator (Can.)

GEORGE DANBY
Courtesy Bangor Daily News

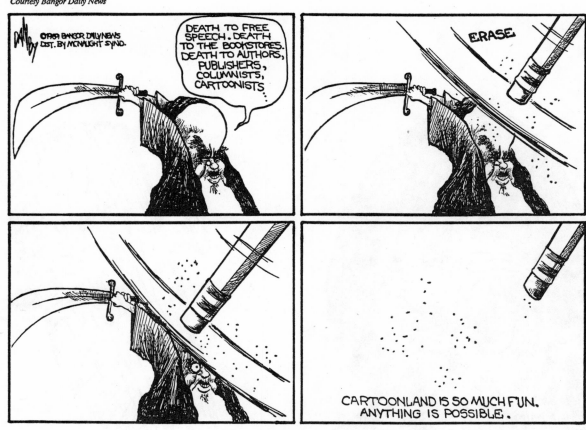

STEVE SACK
Courtesy Minneapolis Star-Tribune

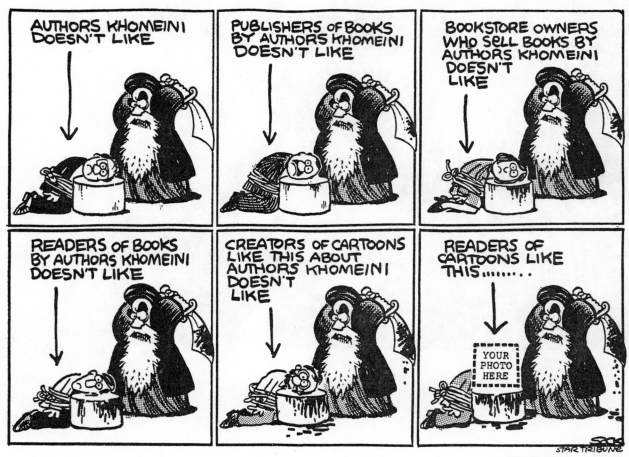

RAY OSRIN
Courtesy Cleveland Plain Dealer

GENTLEMEN, GENTLEMEN, YOU'VE GOT TO REACH OUT TO EACH OTHER.

FRANK EVERS
Courtesy New York Post

WALT HANDELSMAN
Courtesy New Orleans Times-Picayune

61

"IT'S JUST THEIR *FLAG* THAT GETS THEM MAD. . . . YOU CAN
DESECRATE *AMERICANS* ALL YOU WANT! . . ."

"EXPLAIN THE DIFFERENCE BETWEEN 'CHOSEN PEOPLE' AND 'MASTER RACE' AGAIN."

JOHN BRANCH
Courtesy San Antonio Express-News

ALAN VITELLO
Courtesy Denver Catholic Register

(SOMEWHERE IN LEBANON 1989)

SPYDER WEBB
Courtesy Associated Features

GEORGE FISHER
Courtesy Arkansas Gazette

THE NEW ARAFAT...

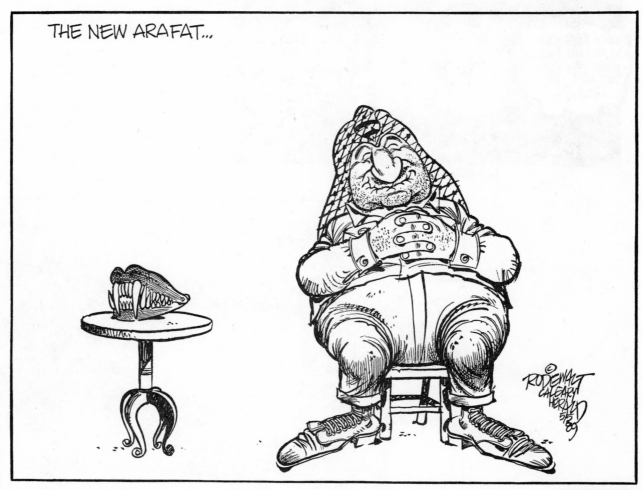

VANCE RODEWALT
Courtesy Calgary Herald

Congress

Congress, to the relief of at least some Americans, enacted little legislation during the first half of the year as the institution found itself embroiled in controversy after controversy.

Following a long, drawn-out investigation, President Bush's nomination of former Texas senator John Tower as secretary of defense was voted down. The House Ethics Committee investigated House Speaker Jim Wright, a Democrat from Texas, for several months. It was alleged that he had accepted $145,000 in improper gifts, that he had failed to report a $100,000 junk bond transaction, and that his wife drew an unearned salary of $18,000 a year from a constituent. Eventually, Wright resigned and the charges were dropped.

Early in the year, Congress attempted to give itself a 51 percent pay raise, but decided to re-think the idea after a public uproar. Later in the year, however, a 33 percent salary increase for House members, government officials, and federal judges was hurriedly pushed though. It was done so quickly that opponents had little time to rally their troops.

During the year Congress passed a sweeping bill to rescue the ailing savings and loan industry. The measure is expected to cost taxpayers tens of billions of dollars. The federal budget totaled 1.2 trillion dollars for the year, with a deficit of $152 billion.

JOHN DEERING
Courtesy Arkansas Democrat

BILL COSTELLO
Courtesy The Diamondback

"That's right — for only $182.50 per day, **YOU** can help balance the budget!"

JACK CORBETT
Courtesy UAW LUPA Newsline

HOSTAGE

PAUL SZEP
Courtesy Boston Globe

Berry's World

JIM BERRY
Courtesy NEA

ROGER SCHILLERSTROM
Courtesy Crain Communications

·THE CANE MUTINY·

ARTHUR BOK
Courtesy Akron Beacon-Journal

TOM CURTIS
Courtesy National Review

"AND NOW, FOR THE DEMOCRATIC VERSION OF THE WAR ON DRUGS . . . "

JACK MCLEOD
Courtesy Army Times

JACK HIGGINS
Courtesy Chicago Sun-Times

JERRY FEARING
Courtesy St. Paul Pioneer Press-Dispatch

MICHAEL THOMPSON
Courtesy St. Louis Sun

PAUL FELL
Courtesy Lincoln Journal

THE PAPER CUT.

HARVEll Greenville News-Piedmont © '89

ROGER HARVELL
Courtesy Greenville News-Piedmont

BILL SANDERS
Courtesy Milwaukee Journal

THE 100 MILLION DOLLAR CATCH

JIM DOBBINS
Courtesy Union Leader (N.H.)

REX BABIN
Courtesy Albany Times-Union

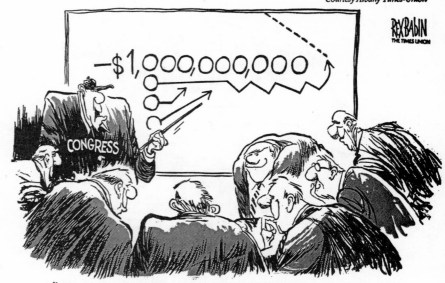

"FAKE TO GRAMM-RUDMAN, PULL THE OLD END RUN, THEN PASS THE BUCK..."

MIKE SMITH
Courtesy Las Vegas Sun

WAYNE STAYSKAL
Courtesy Tampa Tribune

" I THOUGHT HE WAS A MEMBER OF A SPECIAL INTEREST GROUP...
BUT I FOUND OUT HE'S ONLY A VOTER ! "

MIKE SHELTON
Courtesy Orange County Register

DAVID MARTIN
Courtesy Press Publications (Ill.)

73

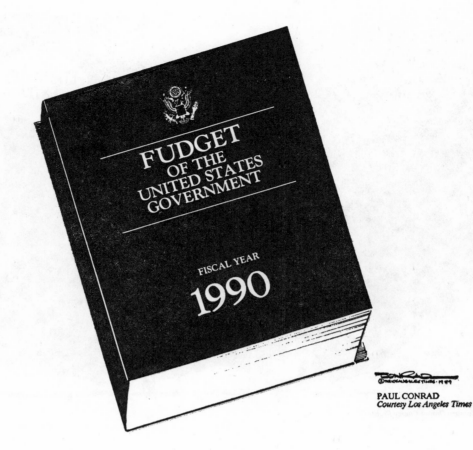

PAUL CONRAD
Courtesy Los Angeles Times

BILL COSTELLO
Courtesy The Diamondback

Scandals

The U.S. Department of Housing and Urban Development (HUD) was a hotbed of scandal during 1989. Two private housing agents who worked with HUD were charged with embezzling some $8 million from sales of government-owned homes and in other business deals. After a year of investigation, evidence showed that under the passive administration of Secretary Samuel Pierce, dubbed "Silent Sam," billions of dollars were diverted from funds intended to help middle-income homeowners and the poor. Instead, the money had gone to highly paid lobbyists, to housing developers, and for fraudulent activities around the country.

Former New York congressman Jack Kemp was appointed to take over the reins at HUD. Kemp immediately set about restructuring the agency's programs and tightening fiscal controls.

The two-month trial of Oliver North concluded on May 4. The former Marine was convicted on three felony accounts relating to the plan to sell arms to Iran. He was acquitted on nine other counts, fined $150,000, placed on probation, and ordered to perform 1,200 hours of public service.

The nomination of former Texas senator John Tower for secretary of defense was rejected by the Senate after a heated partisan battle.

Hotel queen Leona Helmsley, who allegedly had boasted that "only the little people pay taxes," was convicted of tax evasion.

ONE LAST MEDAL

JEFF STAHLER
Courtesy Cincinnati Post

SCAPEGOAT

STEVE LINDSTROM
Courtesy Duluth News-Tribune

JEFF STAHLER
Courtesy Cincinnati Post

JERRY BARNETT
Courtesy Indianapolis News

MIKE SMITH
Courtesy Las Vegas Sun

JOHN TREVER
Courtesy Albuquerque Journal

MIKE SHELTON
Courtesy Orange County Register

ED STEIN
Courtesy Rocky Mountain News

BOB RICH
Courtesy New Haven Register

DRAPER HILL
Courtesy Detroit News

The Price Is Wright

DAN FOOTE
Courtesy Dallas Times-Herald

CHRIS OBRION
Courtesy Potomac News

SANDY CAMPBELL
Courtesy The Tennessean

NEIL GRAHAME
Courtesy Spencer Newspapers

JERRY BUCKLEY
Courtesy Marybeth Cartoons

HELLO, JIMMY... ARE YOU AND ROSALYNN STILL INTO REBUILDING OLD STRUCTURES?

DANA SUMMERS
Courtesy Orlando Sentinel

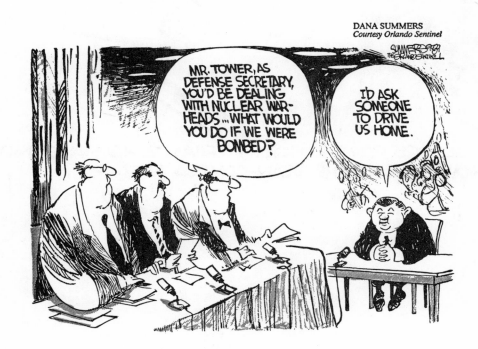

PROSPECTIVE JURORS FOR THE NORTH TRIAL WHO HAVE NO
KNOWLEDGE OF THE IRAN-CONTRA AFFAIR.

PAUL CONRAD
Courtesy Los Angeles Times

NEWS ITEM: NORTH ORDERED TO PERFORM 1,200 HOURS HELPING D.C. YOUTH.

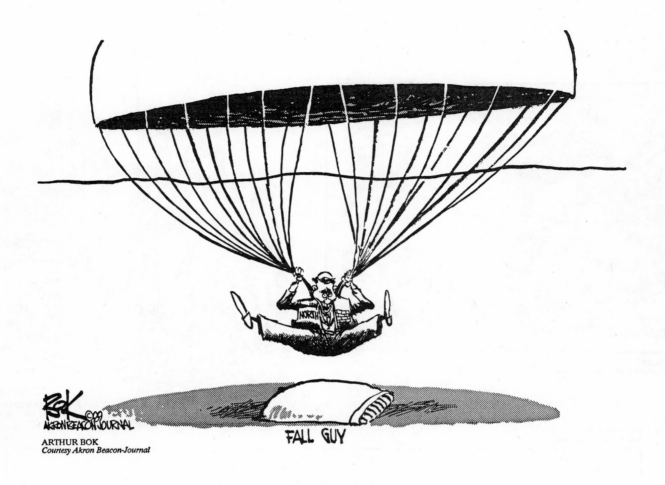

ARTHUR BOK
Courtesy Akron Beacon-Journal

FALL GUY

GENE BASSET
Courtesy Atlanta Journal

SAM PIERCE SLEPT HERE.

The Drug War

Early in the year, President Bush appointed William J. Bennett as director of the national drug control policy. A new campaign was launched against drug trafficking, including a ban on imported semi-automatic rifles. The new policy called for increased spending for law enforcement, as well as for drug education and treatment. At the end of 1989, however, the drug problem continued to grow, indicating that, for the moment at least, the government is fighting a losing battle.

Crack, a smokable, highly addictive, and fairly cheap form of cocaine, was the most common drug being trafficked. There seemed to be an insatiable demand for crack in major American cities, and increasingly larger numbers of dealers were selling crack.

As the U.S. moved to stem the flow of drugs into Florida, the drug barons shifted their operations to Southern California, Texas, New Mexico, and Arizona. Colombia, the source of most cocaine smuggled into the U.S., experienced numerous assassinations among public officials battling the drug dealers. The Colombian government took a tougher stance against the drug cartels after a leading candidate for president was slain by a drug hit squad.

Drug bosses issued a declaration of "total war" against the Colombian government late in the year, but their operations appeared to have been somewhat disrupted by government efforts to eradicate them.

GEORGE DANBY
Courtesy Bangor Daily News

MISS ELVIRA STUMPBERGER TAKES UP THE BUSH ADMINISTRATION SUGGESTION THAT SHE CHASE AWAY LOCAL DRUG DEALERS. MEMORIAL SERVICES NEXT TUESDAY.

JOE LONG
Courtesy Little Falls (N.Y.) Evening Times

ERIC SMITH
Courtesy Annapolis Capital-Gazette

BRUCE PLANTE
Courtesy Chattanooga Times

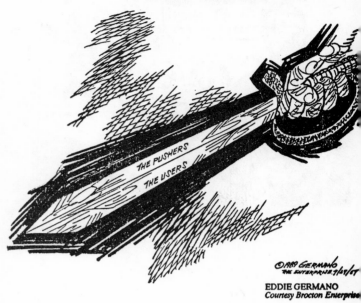

EDDIE GERMANO
Courtesy Brocton Enterprise

CLAY BENNETT
Courtesy St. Petersburg Times

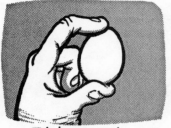

This is your brain...

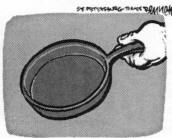

This is drugs...

This is your brain on drugs...

Now, this is the Bill of Rights.

LINDA BOILEAU
Courtesy Frankfort State Journal

JIM LANGE
Courtesy Daily Oklahoman

ED GAMBLE
Courtesy Florida Times-Union

JOHN BRANCH
Courtesy San Antonio Express-News

FRANK CAMMUSO
Courtesy Syracuse Herald-Journal

CHAS FAGAN
Courtesy Ligonier (Pa.) Echo

JEFF KOTERBA
Courtesy Omaha World-Herald

WHAT THE WAR ON DRUGS IS REALLY ABOUT...

VANCE RODEWALT
Courtesy Calgary Herald

WOODSTOCK NOSTALGIA

HY ROSEN
Courtesy Albany Times-Union

MIKE LUCKOVICH
Courtesy Atlanta Constitution

He shoulda known better than to be wearing a "Just Say No" button...

LAMBERT DER
Courtesy Greenville News-Piedmont

SCOTT STANTIS
Courtesy Commercial Appeal

STEVE SCALLION
Courtesy Arkansas Democrat

DAVID HITCH
Courtesy Worcester Telegram and Gazette

STEVE GREENBERG
Courtesy Seattle Post-Intelligencer

VIC HARVILLE
Courtesy Arkansas Democrat

BRUCE BEATTIE
Courtesy Daytona Beach News-Journal

"Our expectations about Star Wars have been scaled back. All it'll protect are defense companies in case of a recession..."

VIC HARVILLE
Courtesy Arkansas Democrat

U.S. Defense

Things did not go well for the U.S. Navy during 1989. In April, a gun turret exploded aboard the battleship *Iowa*, killing 47 sailors during training exercises in the Atlantic. A four-month investigation concluded that the tragedy probably was caused intentionally by a sailor who died in the blast.

Several other serious accidents occurred on naval vessels during the year, and the Navy ordered the first-time-ever suspension of routine operations for 48 hours in order to conduct a fleet-wide safety review.

The defense budget President Bush sent to Congress differed little from the Reagan administration figures, totaling $315.2 billion. The Strategic Defense Initiative (SDI) was slashed by $1.1 billion, however. Development of the Stealth bomber also was slowed because of its high cost of $530 million per aircraft.

Because of the series of unprecedented events in Eastern Europe and the Soviet Union during the year, the Pentagon worried that other areas of defense spending might be cut.

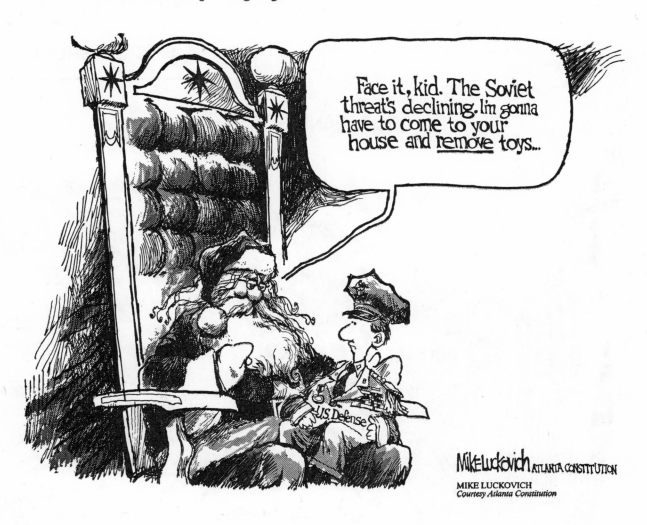

MIKE LUCKOVICH
Courtesy Atlanta Constitution

JEFF BACON
Courtesy Navy Times

Berry's World

STICKER SHOCK

JIM BERRY
Courtesy NEA

THE LEANING TOWER

REX BABIN
Courtesy Denver Post

TIM HARTMAN
Courtesy New Hampshire News Record

JEFF BACON
Courtesy Navy Times

KIRK WALTERS
Courtesy Toledo Blade

CHARLES DANIEL
Courtesy Knoxville Journal

JERRY FEARING
Courtesy St. Paul Pioneer Press-Dispatch

JOHN STAMPONE
Courtesy Salisbury (Md.) Daily Times

CHUCK AYERS
Courtesy Akron Beacon-Journal

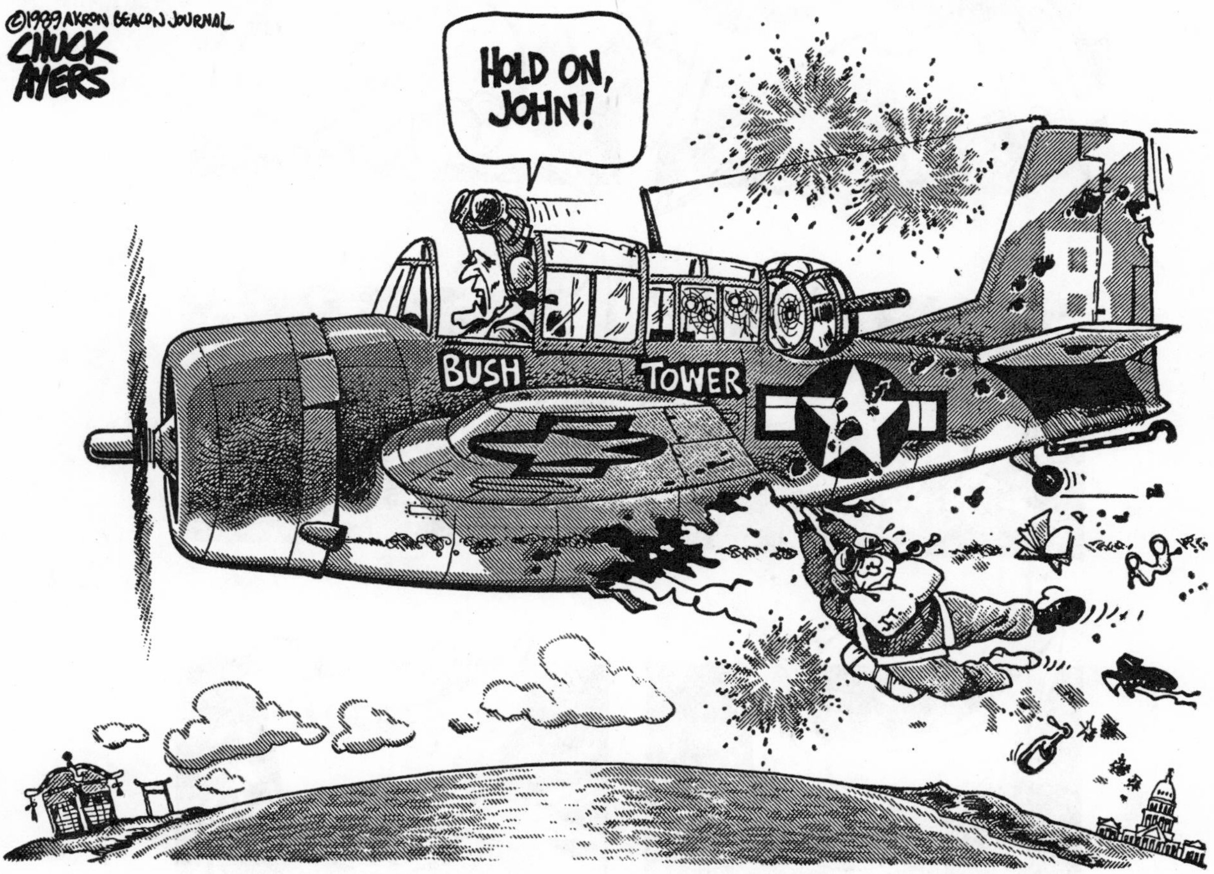
©1989 AKRON BEACON JOURNAL
CHUCK AYERS
HOLD ON, JOHN!
BUSH
TOWER
B

STEVE MCBRIDE
Courtesy Independence (Kan.) Daily Reporter

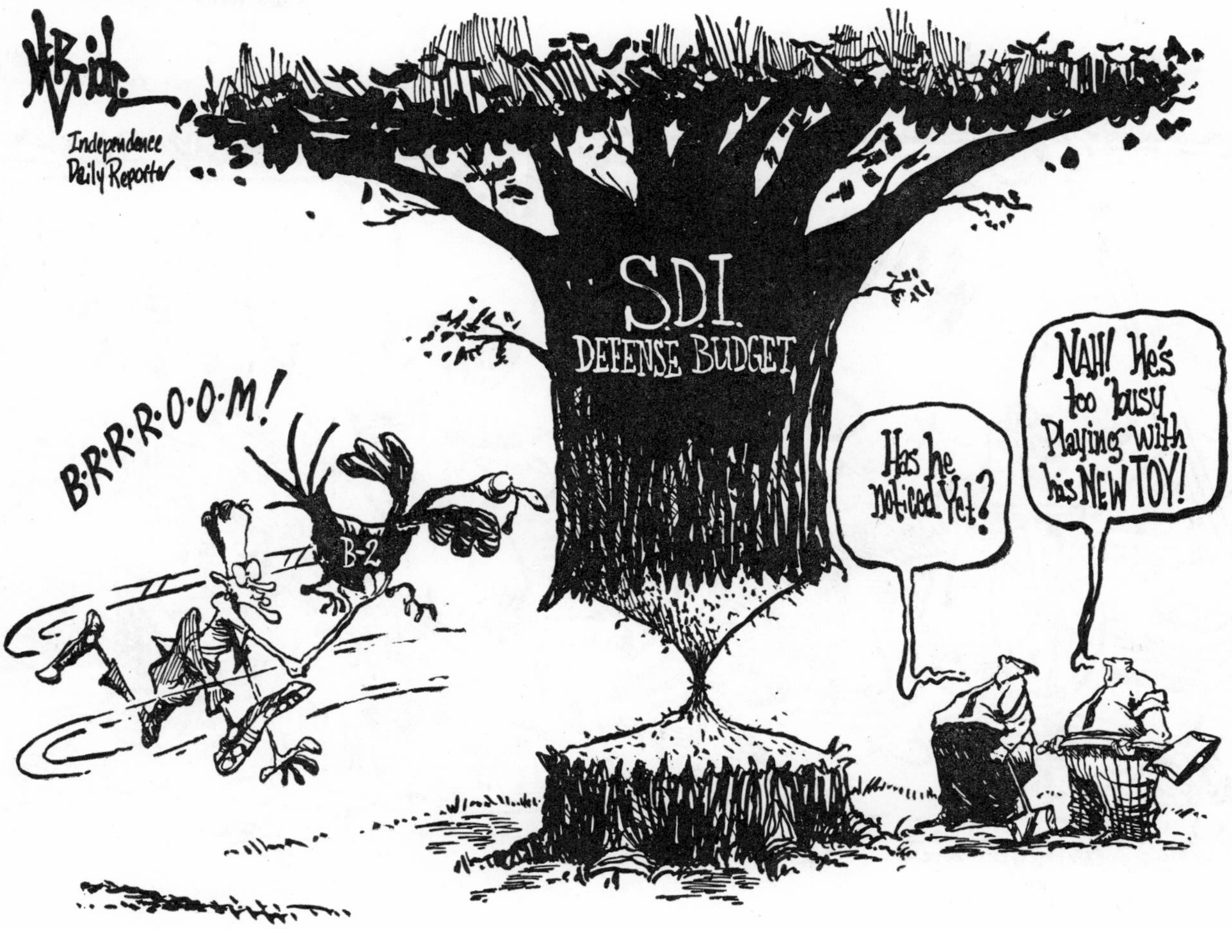
McBride
Independence Daily Reporter
S.D.I.
DEFENSE BUDGET
B-R-R-R-O-O-M!
B-2
Has he noticed yet?
NAH! He's too busy playing with his NEW TOY!

DOUG MACGREGOR
Courtesy USA Today

JERRY FEARING
Courtesy St. Paul Pioneer Press-Dispatch

Disasters

Natural disasters, too, made their presence felt during 1989. In September, Hurricane Hugo roared through the Caribbean, pounding Puerto Rico with winds up to 155 miles per hour. It then headed for the U.S. mainland, striking near Charleston, South Carolina, and devastating much of the region. More than 80 people were killed and tens of thousands were left homeless by the wreckage.

The World Series was interrupted in San Francisco when the Bay Area was shaken by an earthquake measuring 7.1 on the Richter scale. More than 60 people were killed, and damage totaled more than $7 billion. The World Series between the San Francisco Giants and the Oakland Athletics resumed a week later.

A severe earthquake in the Soviet Union early in 1989 took 275 lives, and more than 400 died in a train crash on the trans-Siberian railway. In England, 95 soccer fans were killed in a crowd surge at Hillsborough Stadium in Sheffield.

"IF YOU THINK THAT WAS SOMETHING, WAIT TILL NEXT TIME!"

JAMES LARRICK
Courtesy Columbus Dispatch

EARTHQUAKE

EMIDIO ANGELO
Courtesy Main Line Times

Cruel Blow

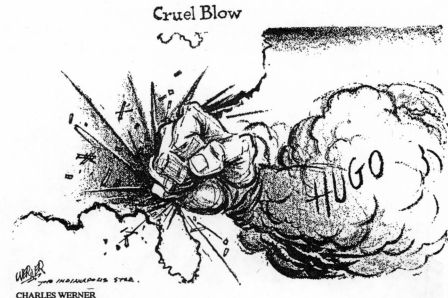

CHARLES WERNER
Courtesy Indianapolis Star

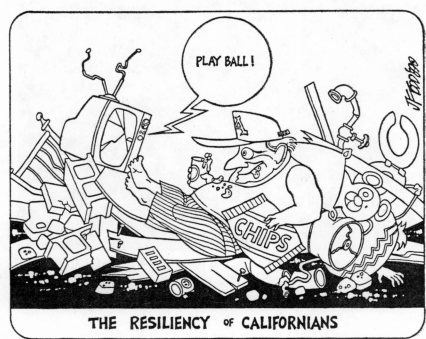

THE RESILIENCY of CALIFORNIANS

JIM TODD
Courtesy Southam Syndicate

CHAN LOWE
Courtesy Fort Lauderdale News/Sun-Sentinel

TOM GIBB
Courtesy Altoona Mirror

"DUE TO THE TERRIBLE EARTHQUAKE HERE IN THE BAY AREA, WE ARE FORCED TO RESCHEDULE TONIGHT'S LECTURE, 'MAN, MASTER OF HIS ENVIRONMENT'..."

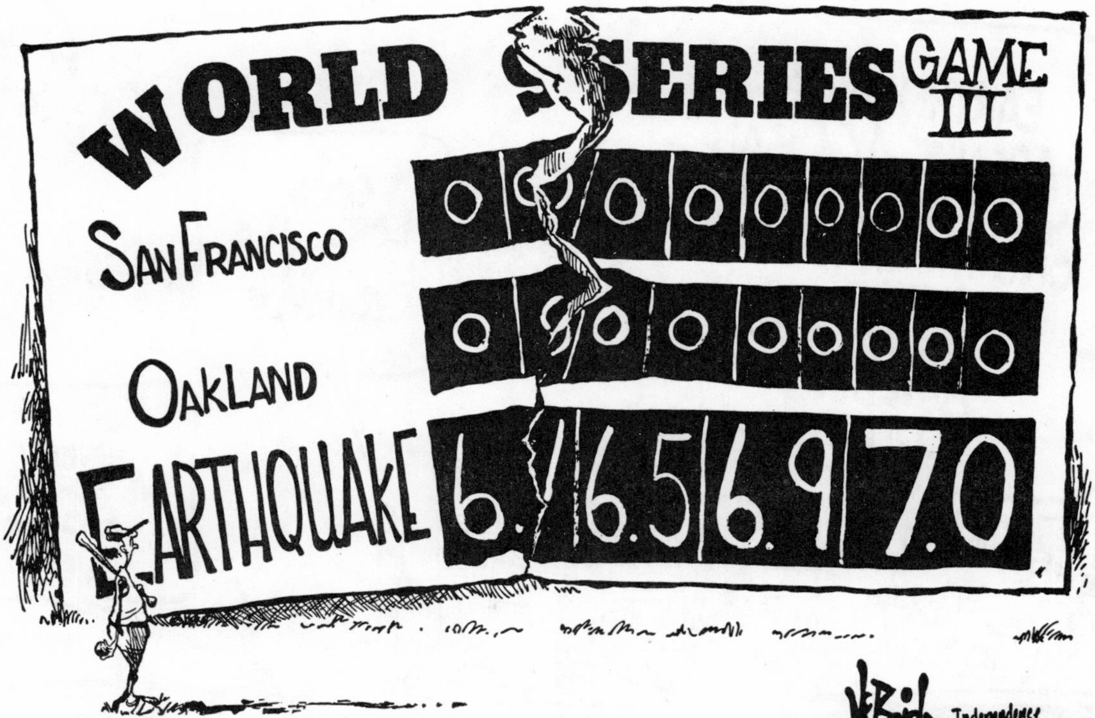
WORLD SERIES
GAME III
SAN FRANCISCO
OAKLAND
EARTHQUAKE 6. 6.5 6.9 7.0
McBride
Independence Daily Reporter

STEVE MCBRIDE
Courtesy Independence (Kan.) Daily Reporter

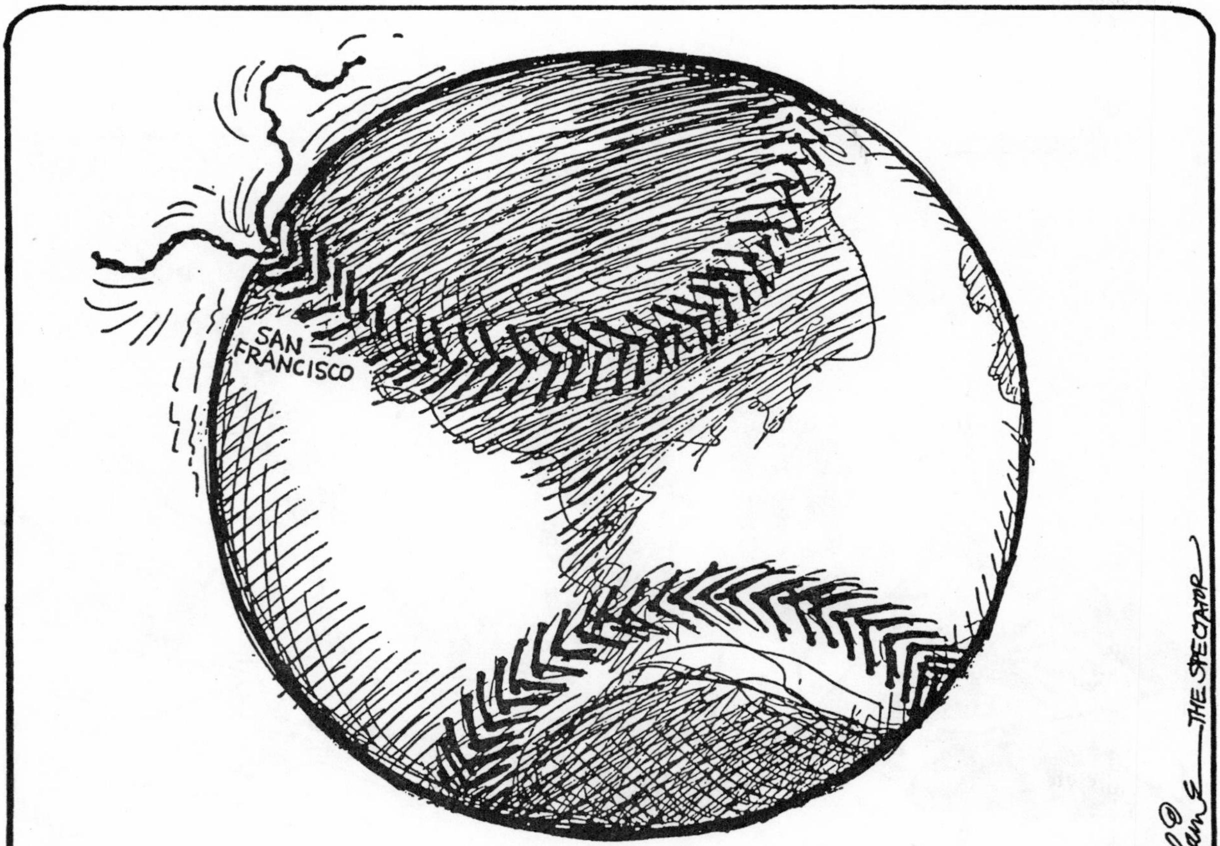
SAN FRANCISCO
NATURE UNRAVELLING
THE SPECTATOR
Blaine

BLAINE
Courtesy The Spectator (Can.)

The Economy

While many economists worried that the U.S. would sink into a depression, 1989 brought continued economic expansion for the seventh consecutive year. The stock market, too, performed well for much of the year. On Friday, October 13, however, the Dow Jones Industrial Average plunged a heart-stopping 190 points. In response, the Federal Reserve announced it would pump money into the banking system as needed, and the following week the market began a spectacular rebound. The economy continued to roll along at a moderate pace, creating an average of more than 200,000 jobs a month.

Despite widespread jitters over Japan's continued economic expansion, the U.S. economy remained in the forefront of world markets. Large American corporations continued to build plants overseas to take advantage of cheaper labor, although in some countries this wage-differential was growing smaller.

It was a difficult year for Sears, Roebuck and Company. The giant chain had instituted a major pricing change in 1988 in an effort to hold its share of retail business in the U.S., but the steady slide nevertheless continued.

Congress raised the minimum wage from $3.35 an hour to $4.25 an hour. It was the first such increase in eight years.

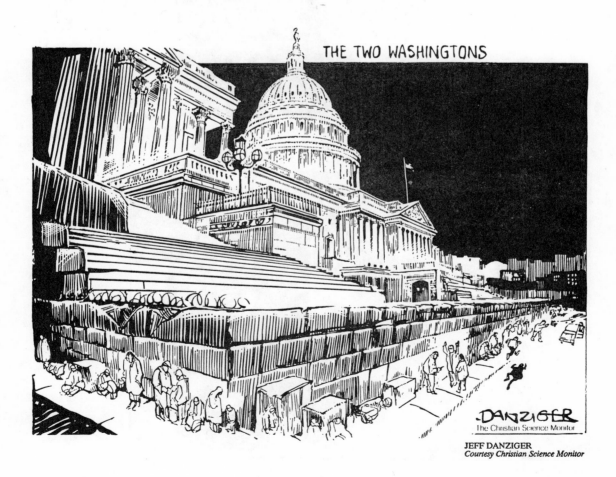

THE TWO WASHINGTONS

DANZIGER
The Christian Science Monitor

JEFF DANZIGER
Courtesy Christian Science Monitor

THE GODDESS OF DEMOCRACY

CHARLES DANIEL
Courtesy Knoxville Journal

KEVIN KALLAUGHER
Courtesy Baltimore Sun

"SCARES THE HECK OUTA ME!"

ART WOOD
Courtesy Farm Bureau News

Now that the Cold War in Europe is over... it's time to turn our attention to the "Cold" War in America.

PETER KOHLSAAT
Courtesy Modern Times Syndicate

TOM BECK
Courtesy Freeport (Ill.) Journal-Standard

Exxon Oil Spill

The *Exxon Valdez*, a giant oil tanker, on March 24 rammed into Bligh Reef near the Alaskan port city of Valdez, dumping some 11 million gallons of crude oil into the clear waters of Prince William Sound. It created an environmental nightmare for Alaska and represented the worst oil spill in U.S. history. More than 30,000 birds and 1,000 sea otters died, along with countless numbers of other sea life. Commercial fishing ground to a halt in the area. At least 1,100 miles of shoreline had been fouled, and winds and tides carried the oil more than 300 miles out to sea.

The *Valdez*, the newest and largest tanker in the Exxon fleet, was commanded by Capt. Joseph Hazelwood, a master mariner who had skippered Exxon ships for 21 years. Tests taken ten hours after the disaster showed Hazelwood had a blood-alcohol level of 0.061 percent, about one-third higher than Coast Guard and company regulations allow. The captain also allegedly violated Exxon policy by leaving the bridge prior to the grounding.

A massive cleanup was undertaken by Exxon, although critics charged the effort was too little too late. After six months of cleanup operations, Exxon pulled out its crews, citing the hazards of winter. The total cost of the oil spill to Exxon is expected to reach $2 billion.

RANDY WICKS
Courtesy The Signal (Calif.)

S. C. RAWLS
Courtesy NEA

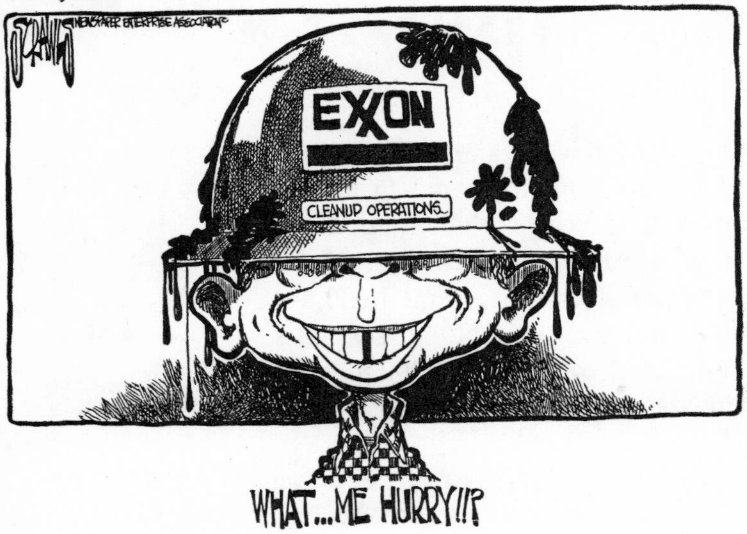
NEWSPAPER ENTERPRISE ASSOCIATION
EXXON
CLEANUP OPERATIONS
WHAT...ME HURRY!!?

GARY VARVEL
Courtesy Indianapolis News

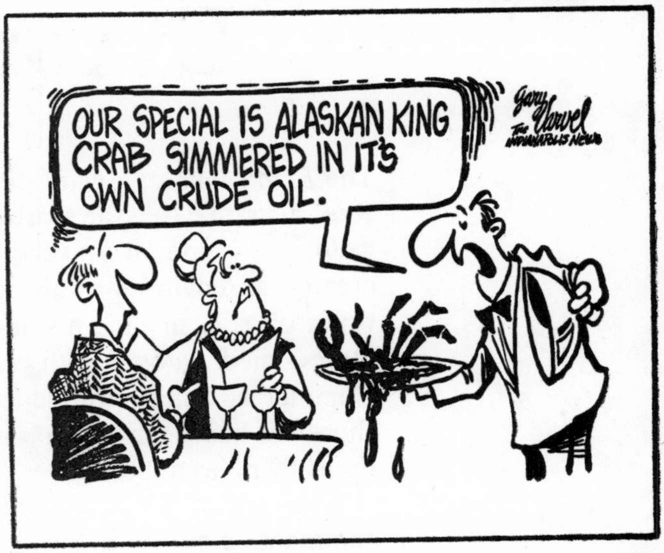
OUR SPECIAL IS ALASKAN KING CRAB SIMMERED IN IT'S OWN CRUDE OIL.
Gary Varvel
The Indianapolis News

BOB JORGENSEN
Courtesy Extra Newspaper Features

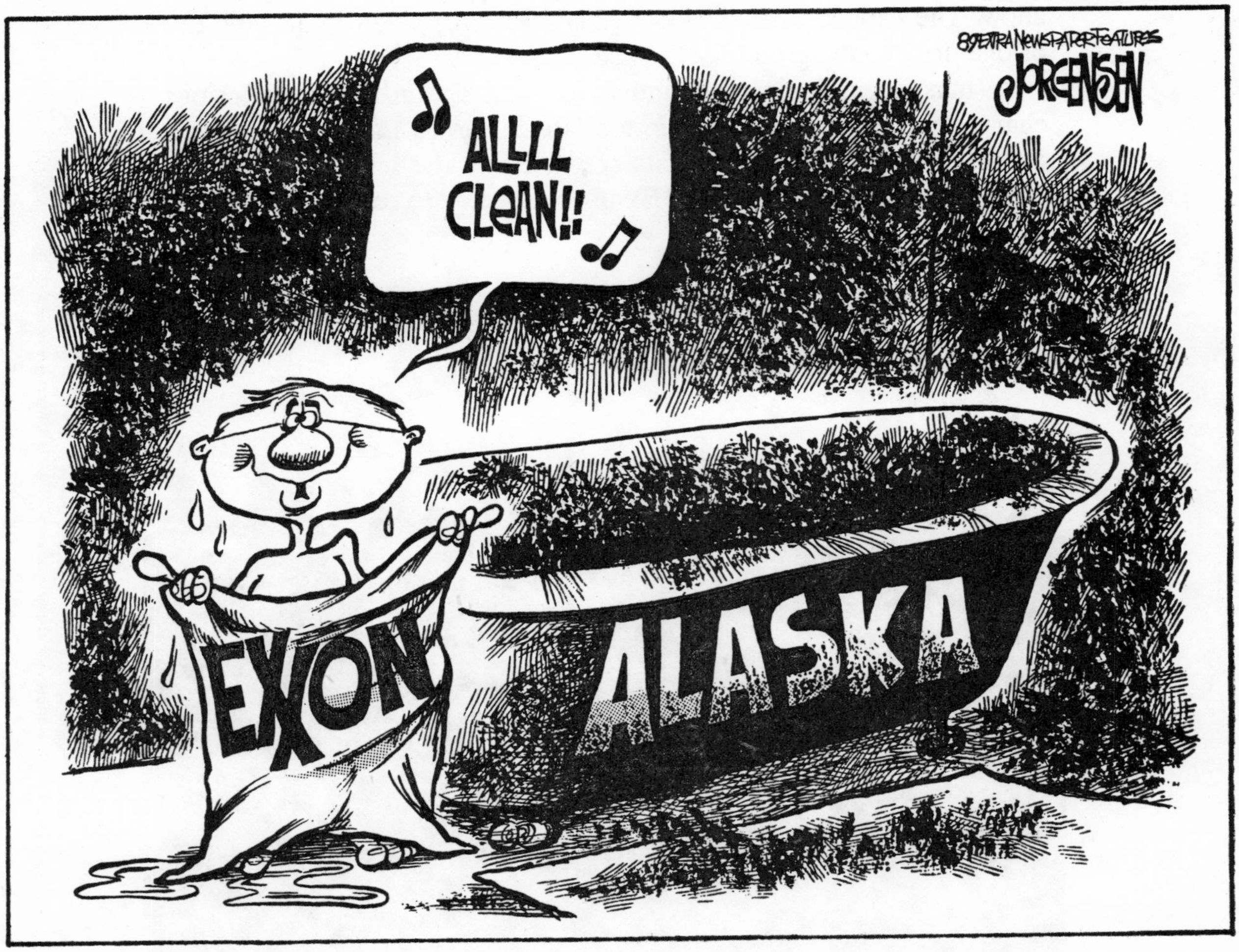
'89 EXTRA NEWSPAPER FEATURES
JORGENSEN
ALLLL CLEAN!!
EXON
ALASKA

ED GAMBLE
Courtesy Florida Times-Union

DAN FOOTE
Courtesy Dallas Times-Herald

MIKE PETERS
Courtesy Dayton Daily News

MIKE LUCKOVICH
Courtesy Atlanta Constitution

JIM TODD
Courtesy Southam Syndicate

REX BABIN
Courtesy Denver Post

LAMBERT DER
Courtesy Greenville News-Piedmont

BRUCE PLANTE
Courtesy Chattanooga Times

Japan

A continuing trade imbalance between Japan and the U.S. which reached $52 billion in 1988 remained a major problem in relations between the two countries. In May, the U.S. cited Japan and two other countries for unfair trade practices, subjecting these countries to possible retaliatory measures if they did not open their markets to American products within 18 months. Japan's markets were regarded as closed to American supercomputers, satellites, and forest products. Talks aimed toward rectifying the trade imbalance began late in the year after Japanese Prime Minister Toshiki Kaifu conferred with President Bush.

Japan's leading real estate company, Mitsubishi Estate, purchased controlling interest in Manhattan's Rockefeller Center and in other properties for $846 million. Previously, Japanese interests had acquired Columbia Pictures and concluded a merger with Firestone Tires.

Emperor Hirohito died on January 7 at the age of 87. He had reigned over Japan for 62 years and saw his country rise from the ashes of defeat in World War II to become an economic giant. He was succeeded by his son, Crown Prince Akihito, who became the 125th emperor of the island nation.

TOM DARCY
Courtesy Newsday

1945: Japan surrenders to America.

1989: America surrenders to Japan.

COMPUTER CHIPS

RICH TENNANT
Courtesy Computerworld

©1989 RICH TENNANT
COMPUTERWORLD
VICTORY GARDEN
SOFTWARE
PCs
AUTOS
CONSUMER ELECTRONICS
JAPANESE BEETLE
SOFTWARE INDUSTRY

JAPANESE HOLDINGS IN AMERICA...
FIRESTONE
ARCO PLAZA
COLUMBIA
ROCKEFELLER CENTER
CBS RECORDS
RAWLS

S. C. RAWLS
Courtesy NEA

ARTHUR BOK
Courtesy Akron Beacon-Journal

AKRON BEACON JOURNAL
©89 BOK
JAPAN
U.S. TRADE POLICY

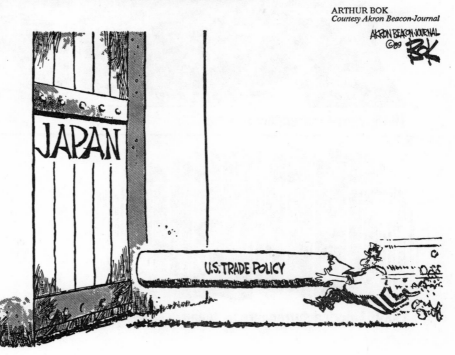

J. ROBERT SHINGLETON
Courtesy Waterbury Republican

JEFF KOTERBA
Courtesy Omaha World-Herald

MICHAEL THOMPSON
Courtesy St. Louis Sun

WAYNE STAYSKAL
Courtesy Tampa Tribune

"I SEE NOW THE VALUE OF ASSAULT RIFLES AND I WISH TO APOLOGIZE FOR THE TERRIBLE THINGS I SAID ABOUT PEOPLE WHO OWN THEM!"

MICHAEL RAMIREZ
Courtesy Daily Sun/Post (Calif.)

Gun Control

In January, a young drifter with a long criminal record killed five children between the ages of 6 and 9 as they played in a Stockton, California, schoolyard. Later in the year, seven workers at a printing plant in Louisville, Kentucky, died when a disgruntled employee on disability leave sprayed bullets throughout the building. Both killers used semi-automatic assault rifles to mow down their victims before turning the weapons on themselves.

President Bush banned imports of these high-power, military-style rifles. The ban, however, did not affect rifles manufactured in the United States, which accounts for 75 percent of all semi-automatic assault rifles sold in the country.

The issue of gun control attracted even more attention in 1989 as law enforcement officials complained they often were outgunned by drug traffickers and other criminals who seemed to have little problem obtaining powerful assault weapons.

GENE BASSET
Courtesy Atlanta Journal

" ISN'T HUNTING A GREAT SPORT?"

MIKE SHELTON
Courtesy Orange County Register

STEVE GREENBERG
Courtesy Seattle Post-Intelligencer

"HE CLAIMS EVERY CITIZEN HAS A RIGHT TO BEAR ARMS."

AL LIEDERMAN
Courtesy Rothco

LAZARO FRESQUET
Courtesy El Nuevo Herald

THE ACCESSORY

CRAIG MACINTOSH
Courtesy Minneapolis Star-Tribune

MIKE KEEFE
Courtesy Denver Post

THE NRA's TROPHY ROOM

Jim Bakker

Fallen television evangelist Jim Bakker stood trial in August on federal charges of conspiracy and fraud. He was accused of conspiring to defraud donors to the PTL (Praise the Lord) Club of $158 million, much of which was spent for huge salaries, bonuses, and extravagant living.

Richard Dortch, one-time executive vice-president of PTL, was the star witness against Bakker, testifying about large bonuses paid to Bakker and his wife Tammy and a $265,000 payment to Jessica Hahn, a church secretary with whom Bakker had a liaison. Dortch also testified he had warned Bakker to stop selling "lifetime partnerships" in Heritage U.S.A. after the theme park became overbooked.

Bakker was found guilty of fraud and conspiracy, and was sentenced to 45 years in prison and fined $500,000.

BLAINE
Courtesy The Spectator (Can.)

JIM BAKKER AND UNINDICTED, CO-CONSPIRATOR

CLYDE WELLS
Courtesy Augusta Chronicle

DANA SUMMERS
Courtesy Orlando Sentinel

HERITAGE U.S.A. TIME SHARE

CHAN LOWE
Courtesy Fort Lauderdale News/Sun-Sentinel

HANK MCCLURE
Courtesy Lawton Constitution

GARY VARVEL
Courtesy Indianapolis News

DOUG MACGREGOR
Courtesy Fort Meyers News-Press

JOHN DEERING
Courtesy Arkansas Democrat

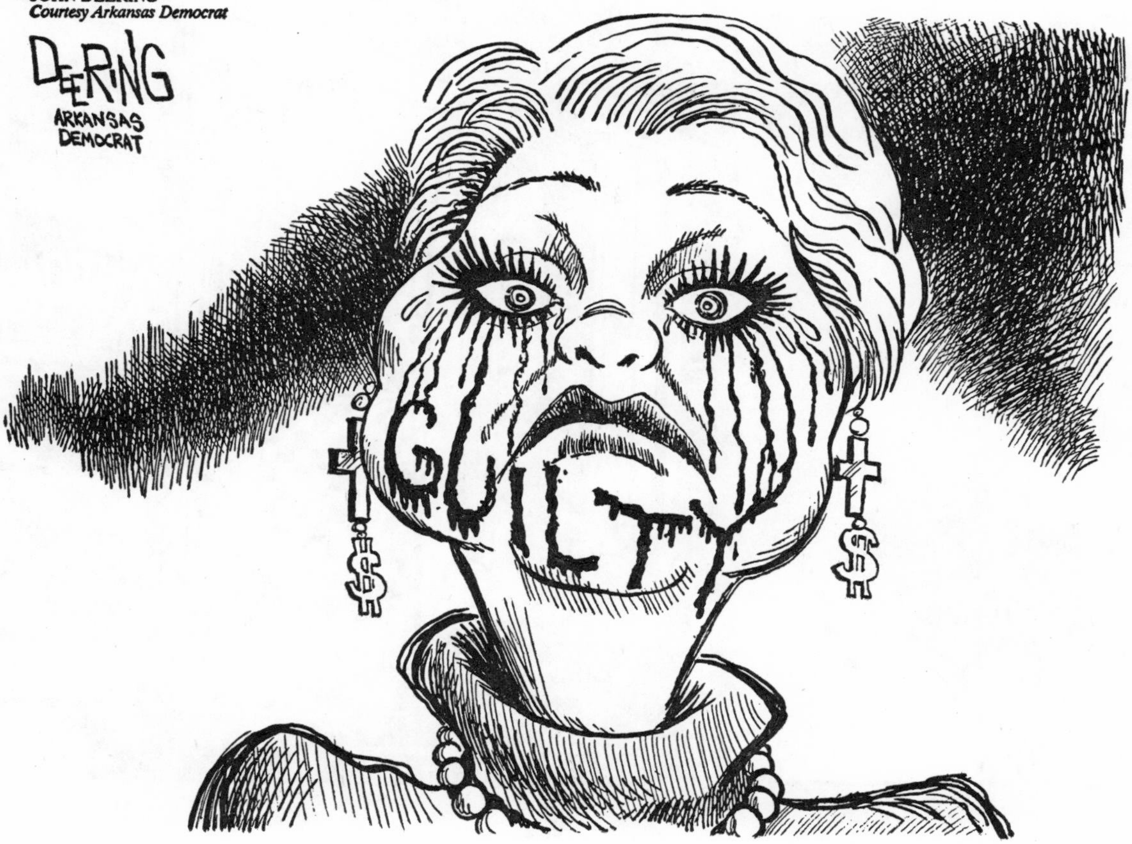
DEERING
ARKANSAS DEMOCRAT
GUILTY

KEVIN SIERS
Courtesy Charlotte Observer

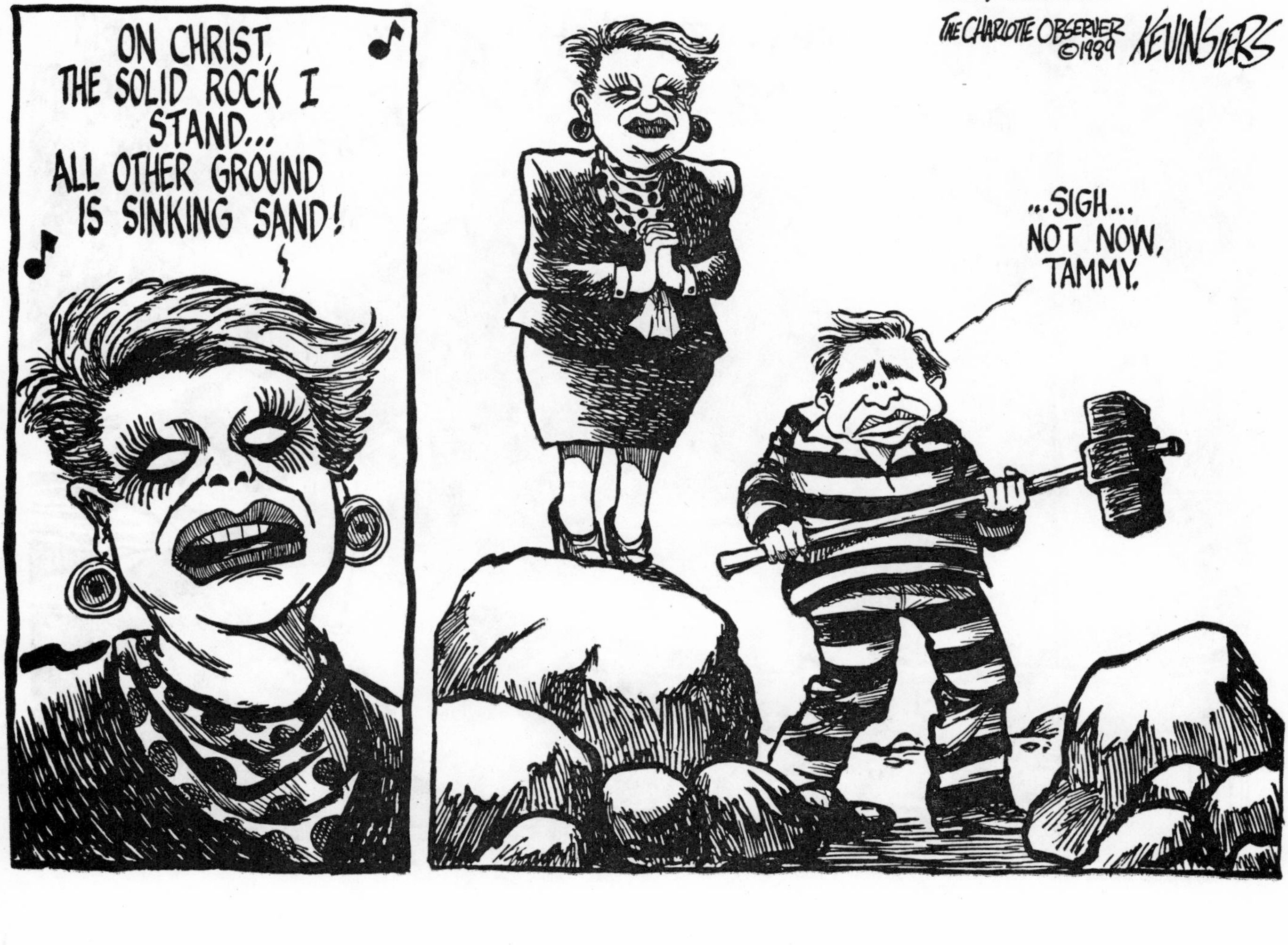
THE CHARLOTTE OBSERVER ©1989 KEVIN SIERS
ON CHRIST, THE SOLID ROCK I STAND... ALL OTHER GROUND IS SINKING SAND!
...SIGH... NOT NOW, TAMMY.

DARKOW
Courtesy San Antonio Light

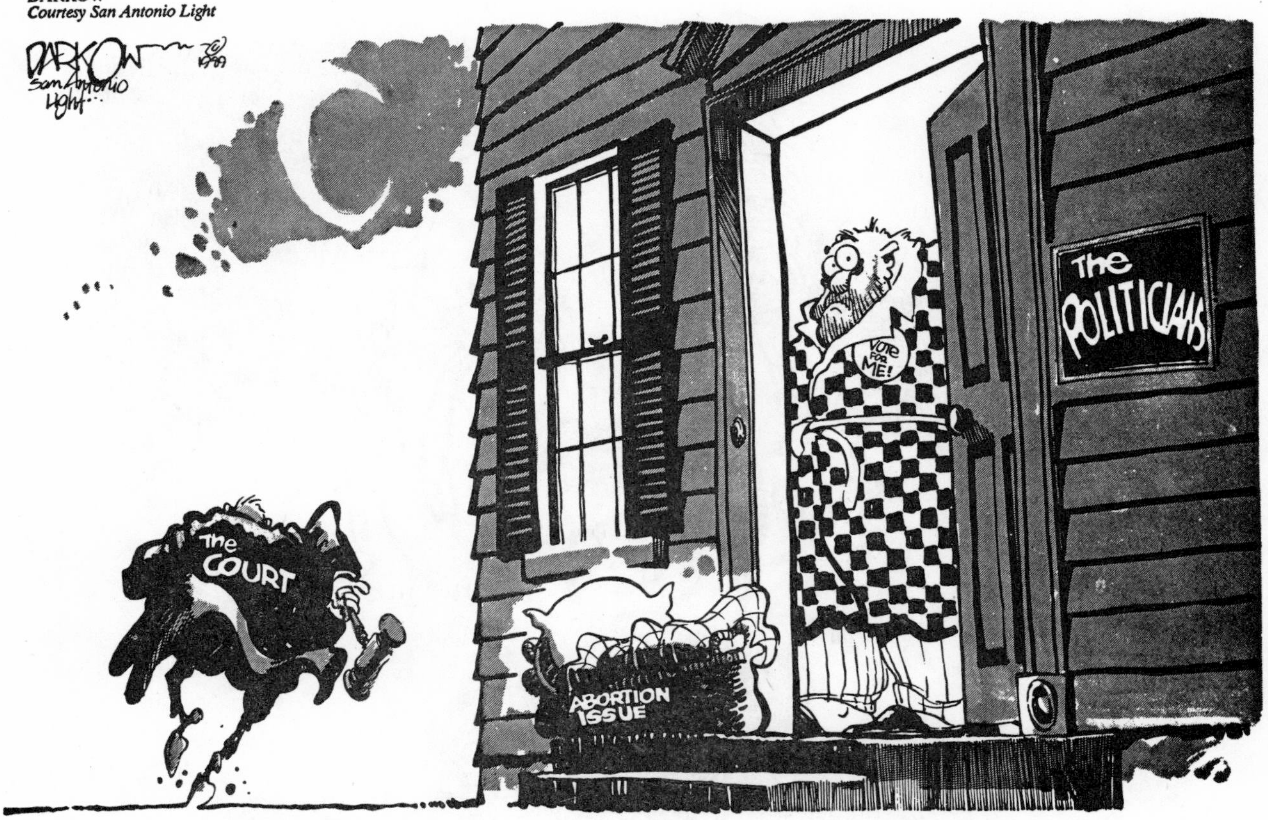
DARKOW San Antonio Light
The POLITICIANS
VOTE FOR ME!
The COURT
ABORTION ISSUE

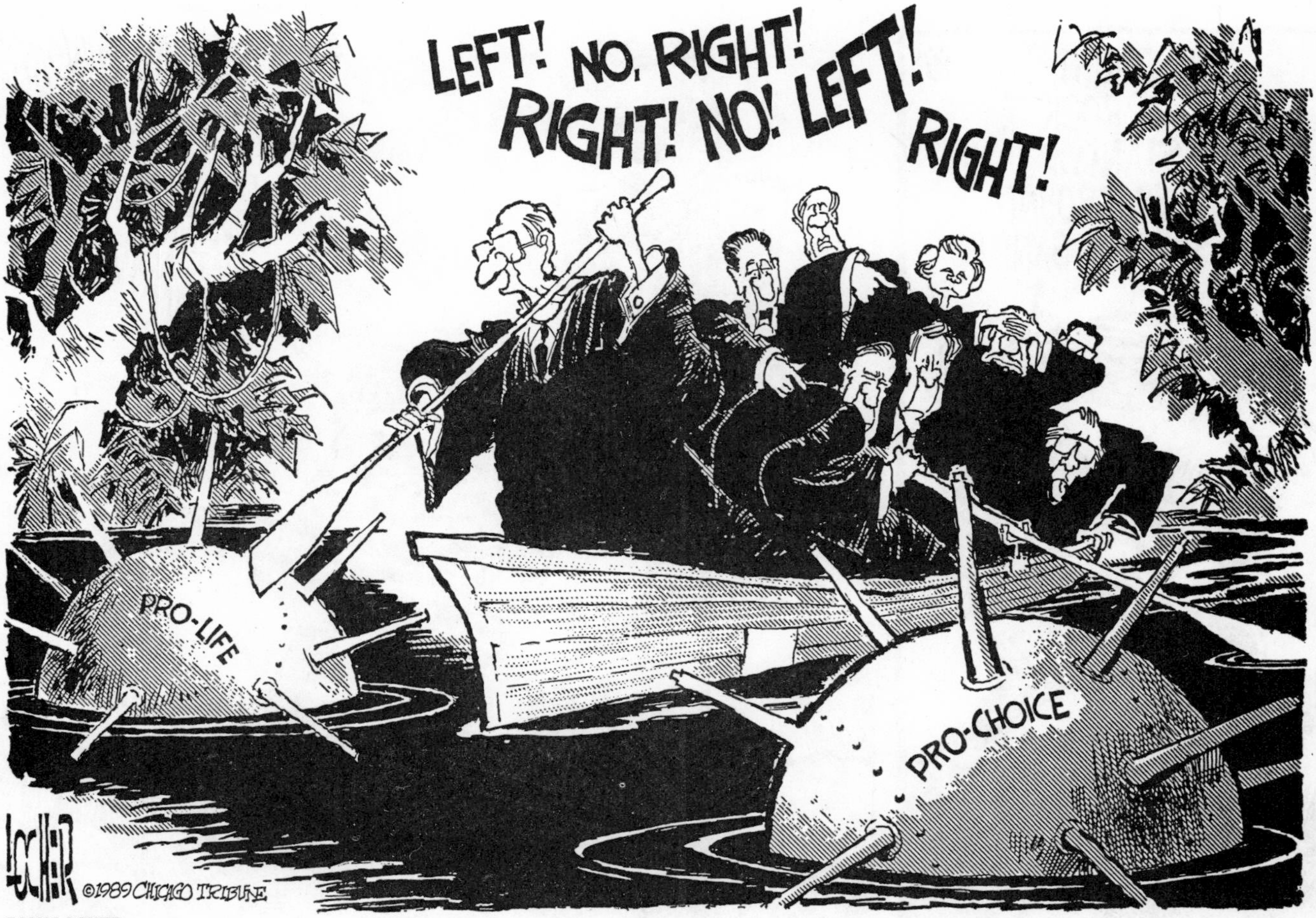
LEFT! NO, RIGHT! RIGHT! NO! LEFT! RIGHT!
PRO-LIFE
PRO-CHOICE
LOCHER ©1989 CHICAGO TRIBUNE

DICK LOCHER
Courtesy Chicago Tribune

U.S. Supreme Court

A new conservative majority on the U.S. Supreme Court, made possible by President Reagan's third appointment, steered that institution to a sharp turn to the right in 1989. Tipping the balance of power was Anthony Kennedy, Reagan's choice to fill the seat vacated by the retirement of Justice Lewis F. Powell, Jr.

In one of its most controversial cases, the court handed to states new authority to decide abortion issues. The new court also put the brakes on affirmative action and declined to ban the death penalty for retarded or young killers.

In cases involving the First Amendment and the separation of church and state, however, the court did not follow the expected conservative trend. The court touched off an uproar among conservatives in June when it ruled 5-4 that the Constitution protects flag-burning as a form of protest. Outraged lawmakers and their constituents were supported by President George Bush who called for a constitutional amendment to outlaw the burning of Old Glory. The Senate, however, voted down the proposed amendment. It was decided that the federal statute could be rewritten to protect the flag without tinkering with the Bill of Rights, and the revised federal statute became law in October.

Several decisions troubled feminists and civil rights advocates who felt the court was turning back the clock on racial and sexual equality.

JERRY LEFLER
Courtesy Ventura County Star-Free Press

UNCLE TOM'S CABIN

ROGER HARVELL
Courtesy Greenville News-Piedmont

THE SAD UNCLE SAM—

OLD GLORY SYMBOLIZES WIDE RANGE OF FREEDOMS!

BURNING FLAG IS FREE SPEECH—SUPREME COURT OVERTURNS CONVICTION FOR PROTEST AT GOP CONVENTION

JOHN SHEVCHIK
Courtesy Valley Tribune (Pa.)

EQUAL·JUSTICE·UNDER·LAW

DENNIS RENAULT
Courtesy Sacramento Bee

PRO-CHOICE ABORTION

SUPREME COURT

FRED MAES
Courtesy Mobile Press Register

BILL SANDERS
Courtesy Milwaukee Journal

THE MILWAUKEE JOURNAL

.... SPEAKING OF DESECRATION !

CHUCK AYERS
Courtesy Akron Beacon-Journal

©1989 AKRON BEACON JOURNAL
CHUCK
AYERS

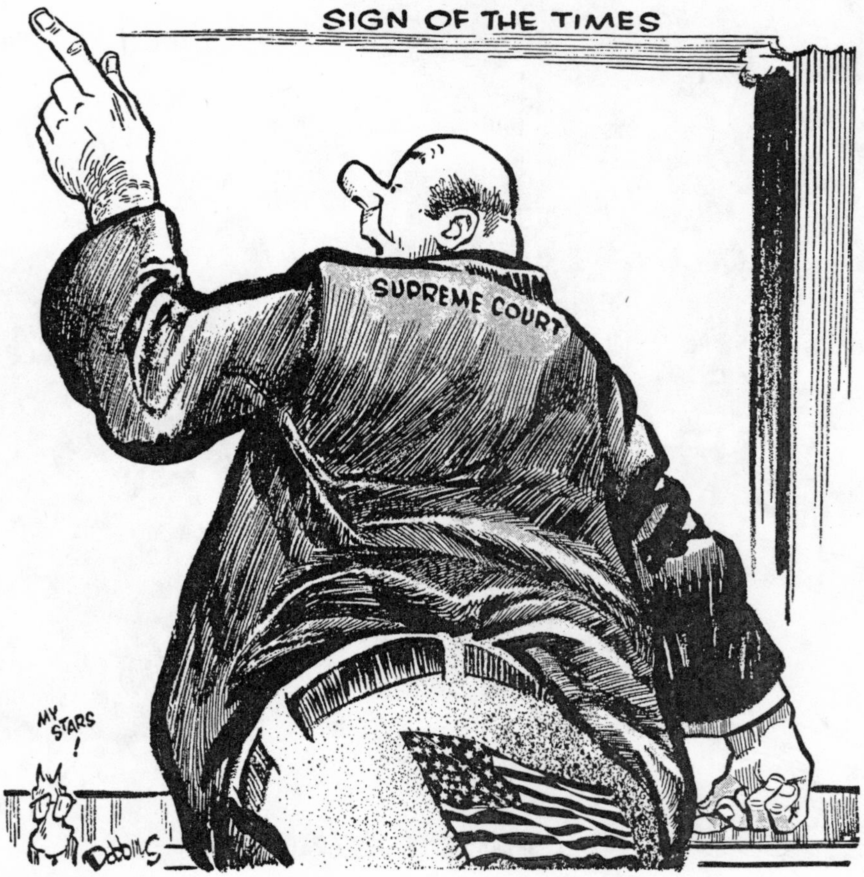
SIGN OF THE TIMES
SUPREME COURT
MY STARS !
DOBBINS

JIM DOBBINS
Courtesy Union Leader (N.H.)

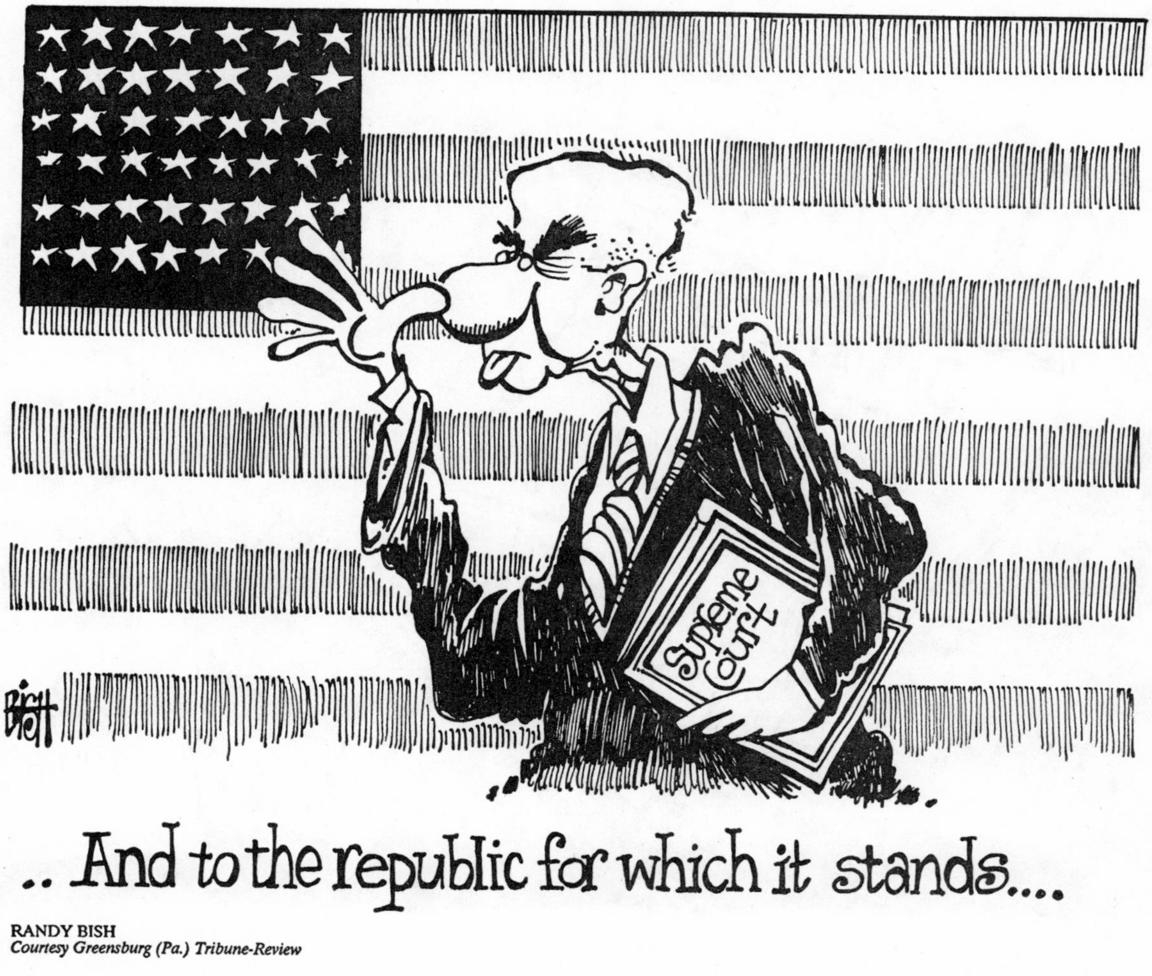
Supreme Court
BISH
.. And to the republic for which it stands....

RANDY BISH
Courtesy Greensburg (Pa.) Tribune-Review

HANK McCLURE
Courtesy Lawton Constitution

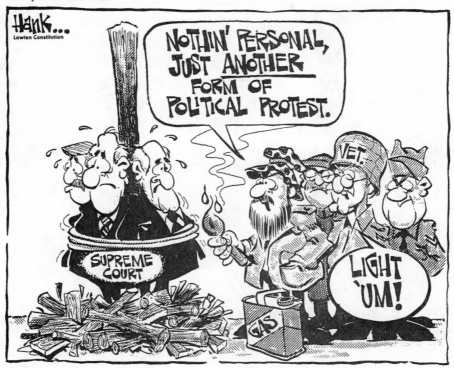

JACK McLEOD
Courtesy Army Times

ROB ROGERS
Courtesy Pittsburgh Press

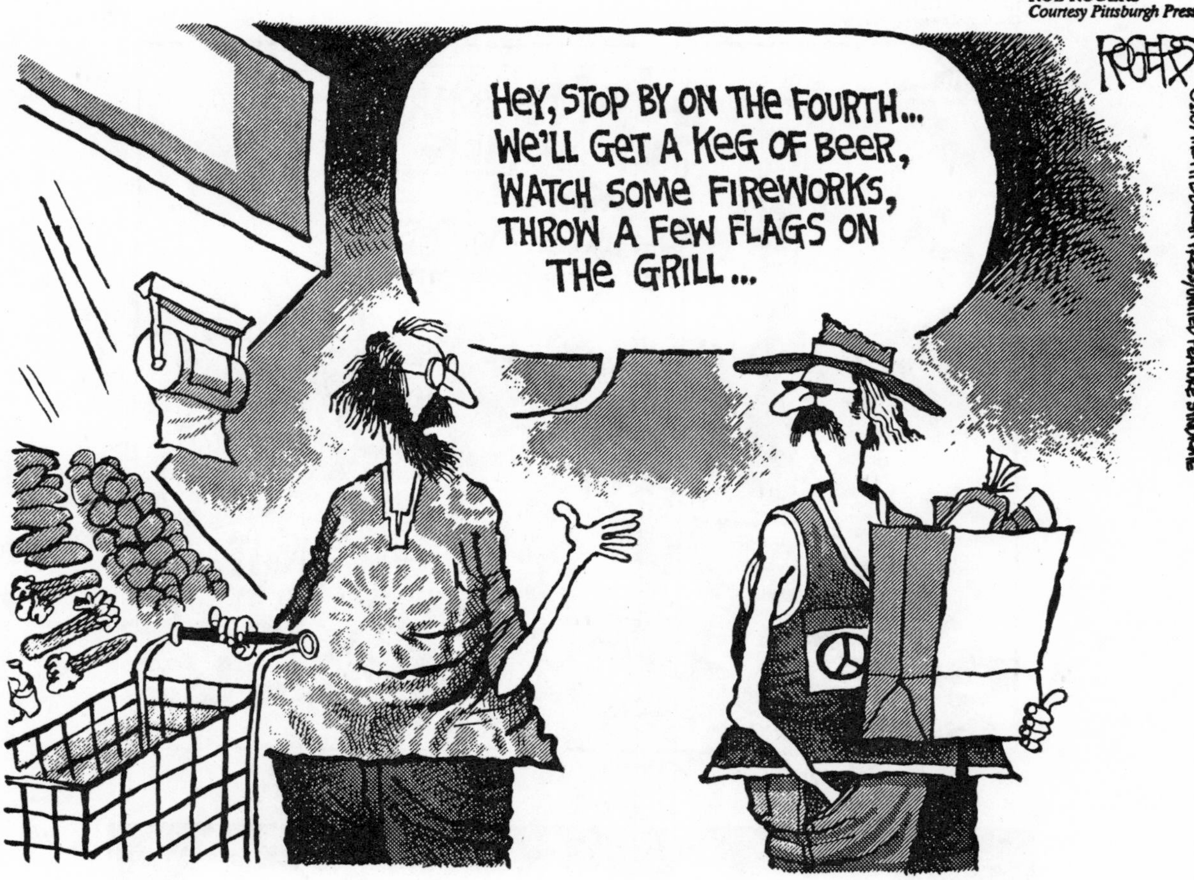
HEY, STOP BY ON THE FOURTH... WE'LL GET A KEG OF BEER, WATCH SOME FIREWORKS, THROW A FEW FLAGS ON THE GRILL...
ROGERS
©1989 THE PITTSBURGH PRESS/UNITED FEATURE SYNDICATE

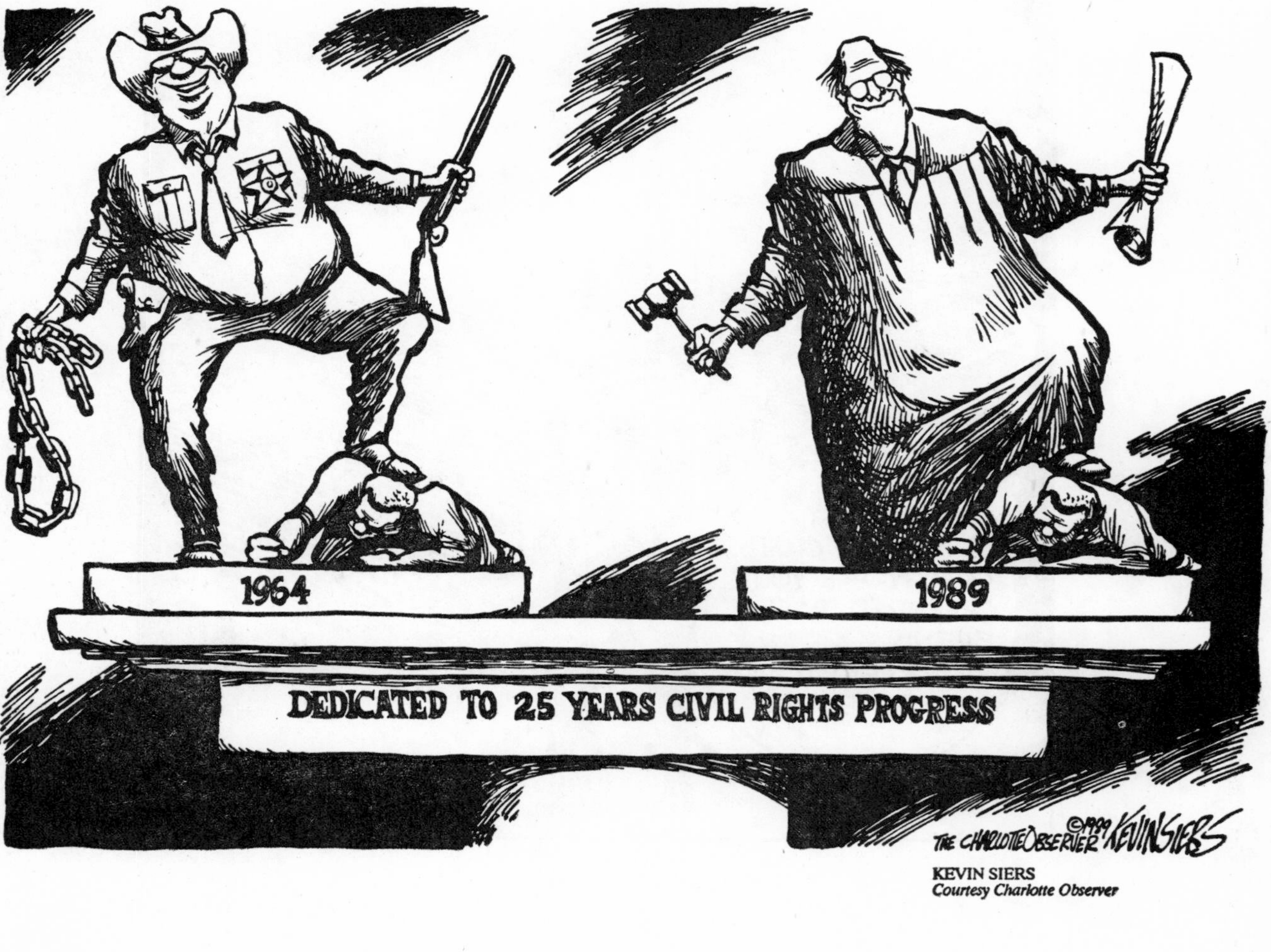
1964
1989
DEDICATED TO 25 YEARS CIVIL RIGHTS PROGRESS
THE CHARLOTTE OBSERVER ©1989 KEVIN SIERS

KEVIN SIERS
Courtesy Charlotte Observer

JERRY BUCKLEY /
Courtesy Marybeth Cartoons

CHRIS OBRION
Courtesy Potomac News

AMERICAN PUBLIC OPINION:

A

TRAITOROUS RADICAL PUNK WHO OUGHT TO BE THROWN IN JAIL OR SHOT

B

HEROIC, PATRIOTIC STUDENT-REFORMER BRUTALLY JAILED OR SHOT FOR EXPRESSING BELIEFS

BOB ENGLEHART
Courtesy Hartford Courant

"IT'S A STRANGE PHENOMENON OF THE EIGHTIES. WHEN YOU GET PREGNANT, YOU BECOME INVISIBLE."

JERRY HOLBERT
Courtesy Boston Herald

Abortion

One of the major issues of the day led to a dramatic confrontation between abortion rights groups and anti-abortion forces following a U.S. Supreme Court ruling on July 3. The court, in Webster *v.* Reproductive Health Services, upheld a Missouri law restricting a woman's right to an abortion.

The ruling was seen as critical by pro-abortion advocates because it was the first abortion case to be heard by the court since President Reagan appointed two conservative justices, Antonin Scalia and Anthony Kennedy.

Many saw the decision as a vehicle the Bush administration might try to use to overturn the 1973 Roe *v.* Wade ruling that essentially legalized abortion nationwide.

In upholding a state's right to restrict abortion, the court reserved final decisions to the fifty state legislatures. President Bush supported the Webster decision and called for action "to restore to the people the ability to protect the unborn."

ABORTION ISSUE
Gill Fox
WESTPORT NEWS

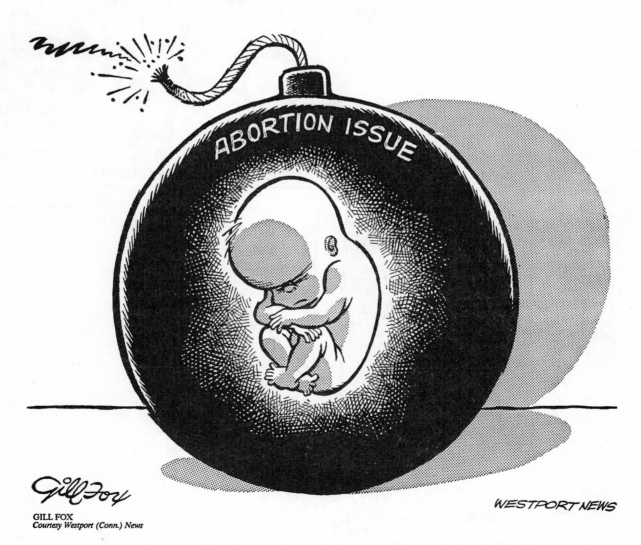

GILL FOX
Courtesy Westport (Conn.) News

WILL O'TOOLE
Courtesy All About Issues Magazine

WHICH ONE IS THE PRO-LIFER?

BRUCE BEATTIE
Courtesy Daytona Beach News-Journal

JERRY LEFLER
Courtesy Ventura County Star-Free Press

"I support abortion in the case of rape, incest, or if my political life is in danger."

JOHN SLADE
Courtesy Louisiana Weekly

JOHN TREVER
Courtesy Albuquerque Journal

JOHN KNUDSEN
Courtesy The Tidings (Calif.)

Sports

Pete Rose, manager of the Cincinnati Reds and a likely Hall of Famer, was banned from baseball for life in 1989 by Commissioner Bartlett Giamatti. It was alleged that between 1985 and 1987 Rose regularly bet on baseball games, including games involving his own team. Rose denied having ever bet on baseball games, but admitted in November that he was receiving counseling for a gambling problem.

Known as "Charlie Hustle" for his all-out style of playing, Rose holds an admirable place in Major League recordbooks. His records include: most hits, 4,256; most at bats, 14,053; most games played, 3,562; 16 All-Star Game appearances; 10 seasons with 200 or more hits; the longest hitting streak in National League history, 44 games; and three National League batting championships.

Rose has a right to apply for reinstatement after one year.

Other personal foibles rocked baseball during the year. Wade Boggs, star third baseman of the Boston Red Sox, was the object of a law suit filed by Margo Adams, allegedly his mistress. Former Dodger all-star Steve Garvey was hit by a breach-of-promise suit filed by an ex-girl friend. And Oakland Athletics slugger Jose Canseco had several run-ins with the police.

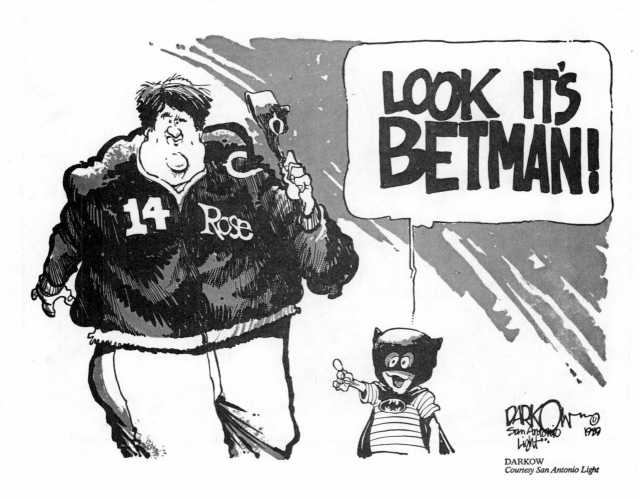

DARKOW
Courtesy San Antonio Light

BOB RICH
Courtesy New Haven Register

BRIAN DUFFY
Courtesy Des Moines Register

DAN FOOTE
Courtesy Dallas Times-Herald

CLYDE WELLS
Courtesy Augusta Chronicle

JERRY BARNETT
Courtesy Indianapolis News

EDD ULUSCHAK
Courtesy Miller Services

DICK GIBSON
Courtesy Thomson News Service

Canada

Canadian sprinter Ben Johnson was stripped of the gold medal he won at the 1988 Seoul Olympics after testing positive for steroid use. An inquiry conducted in June by Justice Charles Dubin found that many other sports figures had been using steroids in preparation for international amateur sports events.

Canadian Finance Minister Michael Wilson found himself in hot water because of a huge budget deficit caused by government spending policies. He planned a 9 percent national goods and services tax to increase revenues, but his proposal drew strong opposition from both Liberals and New Democrats. After much discussion, the idea was left hanging.

The Canadian national rail system (ViaRail) was cut back sharply during the year, with 2,761 workers being laid off. Transport Minister Benoit Bouchard announced in October that a royal commission would study Canada's future transportation needs.

The Meech Lake Accord, ratified by all Canadian provinces except New Brunswick and Manitoba, was designed to bring Quebec into the modern constitutional family by giving more power to the provinces and special powers to Quebec.

The government also applied pressure on industry to hire more minorities regardless of individual qualifications.

M. R. TINGLEY
Courtesy London Free Press

DICK GIBSON
Courtesy Thomson News Service

DICK GIBSON
Courtesy Thomson News Service

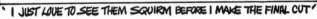

JIM TODD
Courtesy Southam Syndicate

Environment

Scientists confirmed in 1989 that the ozone is being depleted more rapidly than previously had been thought. An international agreement developed by several nations took effect on January 1 and seeks to curb the destruction of this important protective layer.

Scientists also continued to study the 1988 drought and various factors in an effort to determine whether what appears to be a global warming trend known as the greenhouse effect is real, or if the earth's temperature is merely fluctuating.

During the summer, President Bush proposed a variety of new clean-air measures. As air pollution increased, automakers and oil companies stepped up research into cleaner-burning fuels. A new study concluded that major Mayan Indian sites in southern Mexico and Guatemala are being destroyed by acid rain. The source of such pollution was identified as Gulf Coast oil fields operated by Pemex, Mexico's national oil company.

The problem of what to do about garbage continued to grow. Landfills were full, and many locations that had been used as dumping sites were no longer available.

JIM BORGMAN
Courtesy Cincinnati Enquirer

THE BURNING OF THE RAIN FORESTS

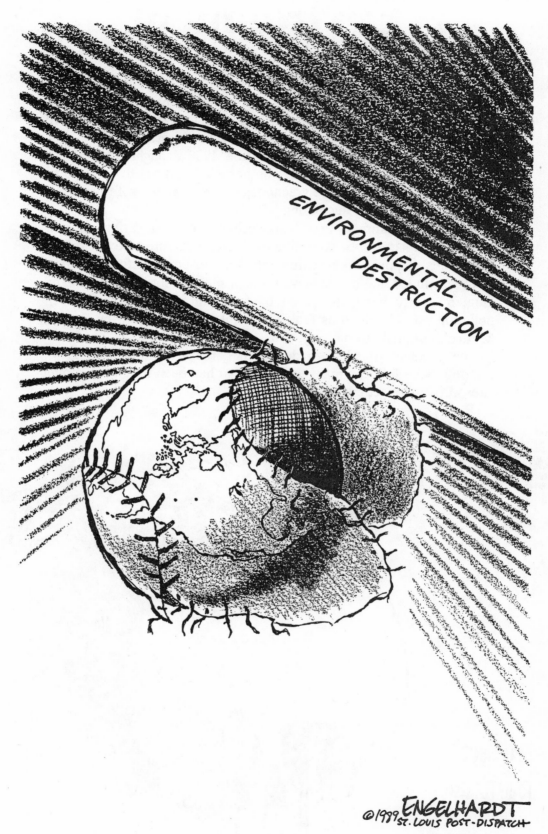

ENVIRONMENTAL DESTRUCTION

Tearing The Hide Off

TOM ENGELHARDT
Courtesy St. Louis Post-Dispatch

BUBBA FLINT
Courtesy Fort Worth Star-Telegram

ETTA HULME
Courtesy Fort Worth Star-Telegram

"WE TAKE THE VIEW THAT IF YOU CAN'T STAND THE POLLUTION, YOU SHOULD STAY OUT OF THE ENVIRONMENT."

ED STEIN
Courtesy Rocky Mountain News

BRIAN DUFFY
Courtesy Des Moines Register

ALAN KING
Courtesy Ottawa Citizen

'REMEMBER WHEN THAT FELLOW USED TO BE JUST A JOKE IN A CARTOON?..'

RANDY BISH
Courtesy Greensburg (Pa.) Tribune-Review

Level with me, Doc...Will I make it to the beach before that syringe?

ED COLLEY
Courtesy Carver Citizen (Plymouth, Mass.)

ALAN KING
Courtesy Ottawa Citizen

TOM BECK
Courtesy Freeport (Ill.) Journal-Standard

DAVID MARTIN
Courtesy Press Publications (Ill.)

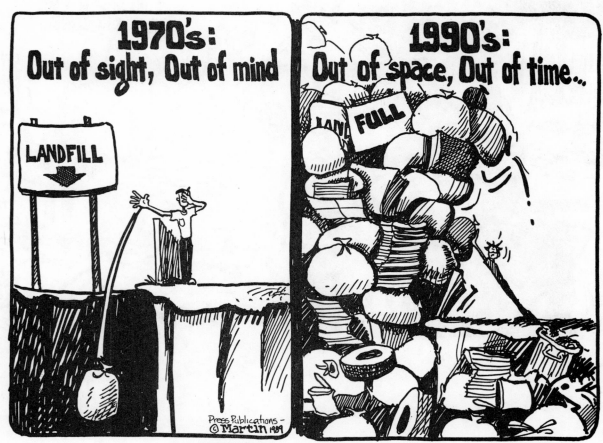

M. R. TINGLEY
Courtesy London Free Press

JOHN KOVALIC
Courtesy Wisconsin State Journal

JOE HELLER
Courtesy Green Bay Press-Gazette

"YA KNOW CONGRESSMAN, MAYBE WE SHOULD ADD AN AMENDMENT ONTO THAT FLAG DESECRATION LAW."

BOB DORNFRIED
Courtesy Rothco

ROGER SCHILLERSTROM
Courtesy Crain Communications

JIMMY MARGULIES
Courtesy Houston Post

Health

A law to provide health care in cases of catastrophic illness among the elderly went into effect in January. It was intended to protect older Americans from the huge costs of extended illness. The measure drew a storm of protest, however, from potential beneficiaries who complained of the cost. The plan was to be financed by a 15 percent surtax borne entirely by senior citizens, rather than by all taxpayers. The cost more than doubled early estimates, and Congress was deluged with mail from angry senior citizens before repealing the law late in the year.

After eight years of the AIDS epidemic, reported cases in the U.S. numbered more than 100,000 in 1989, including 65,000 deaths. The World Health Organization reported 500,000 cases worldwide and estimated that up to 20 million people are infected with the deadly virus. Prospects for finding a cure for the disease were still poor, but research continued.

In March, small quantities of cyanide were found in Chilean grapes in Philadelphia. All Chilean fruit imports were banned temporarily, and growers and exporters suffered losses totaling $240 million. Communist-backed terrorists were blamed with tampering with the fruit.

U.S. Surgeon General C. Everett Koop resigned late in 1989. The controversial Koop declared in one of his last health reports that almost half of all Americans who have ever smoked have kicked the habit.

ROGER HARVELL
Courtesy Greenville News-Piedmont

BOB STAAKE
Courtesy Easy Reader (Los Angeles)

TOM DARCY
Courtesy Newsday

1959: 'Name your poison!'

1989: 'Name your poison!'

MICHAEL RAMIREZ
Courtesy Daily Sun/Post (Calif.)

ART HENRIKSON
Courtesy Des Plaines Daily Herald

JOE HOFFECKER
Courtesy Cincinnati Business Courier

STEVE ARTLEY
Courtesy Agri News

HEAVENLY SLAPSTICK

EDDIE GERMANO
Courtesy Brocton Enterprise

BOB ENGLEHART
Courtesy Hartford Courant

In Memoriam

Death claimed a number of the world's notables during the year, including performers Lucille Ball, Bette Davis, Jim Backus, Sir Lawrence Olivier, and Mel Blanc; Soviet dissident Andrei Sakharov; artist Salvador Dali; baseball commissioner Bartlett Giamatti; Russian diplomat Andrei Gromyko; Japanese Emperor Hirohito; and the Ayatollah Khomeini of Iran.

In addition, the world remembers the Chinese students who, in the face of death, shook the foundations of government tyranny.

M. R. TINGLEY
Courtesy London Free Press

EDDIE GERMANO
Courtesy Brocton Enterprise

STEVE SACK
Courtesy Minneapolis Star-Tribune

...and Other Issues

The problem of aging aircraft became the focus of attention during 1989 after a number of planes suffered apparent structural failure, causing many fatalities. In perhaps the most dramatic incident, a cargo door popped open, ripping a huge hole in a United Airlines 747 over the Pacific Ocean. Nine passengers were sucked to their deaths through the opening. The tail-mounted engine of a DC-10 exploded in flight and, although essential hydraulic controls were wrecked by the blast, the pilot managed to crash land the plane at Sioux City, Iowa, saving many lives.

In August, after having traveled 4.4 billion miles, Voyager 2 completed a 12-year probe of the outer solar system. The spacecraft sent back stunning pictures of the planet Neptune before proceeding out of the solar system.

The art world was rocked by controversy in June when the prestigious Corcoran Gallery of Art cancelled an exhibit featuring photographs deemed to be "obscene or indecent." Senator Jesse Helms of North Carolina introduced a bill to bar federal funds for the support of such art.

David Dinkins became the first black mayor of New York, and rumors spread that long-missing labor leader Jimmy Hoffa was buried in concrete in New York's Shea Stadium. Crime and drugs continued to pose major problems for the nation's schools, and President Bush and U.S. governors held a summit to seek major educational reforms.

S. C. RAWLS
Courtesy NEA

DAVE SATTLER
Courtesy Lafayette Journal Courier

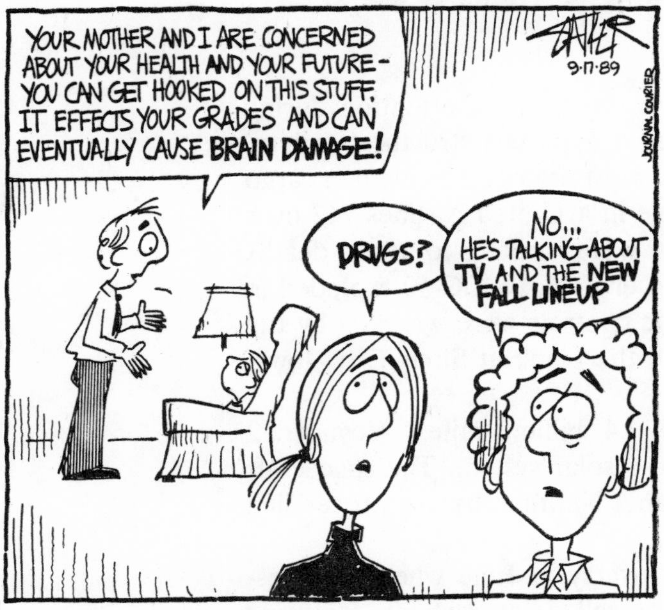

YOUR MOTHER AND I ARE CONCERNED ABOUT YOUR HEALTH AND YOUR FUTURE - YOU CAN GET HOOKED ON THIS STUFF. IT EFFECTS YOUR GRADES AND CAN EVENTUALLY CAUSE BRAIN DAMAGE!
DRUGS?
NO... HE'S TALKING ABOUT TV AND THE NEW FALL LINEUP
9-17-89
JOURNAL COURIER

GARY VARVEL
Courtesy Indianapolis News

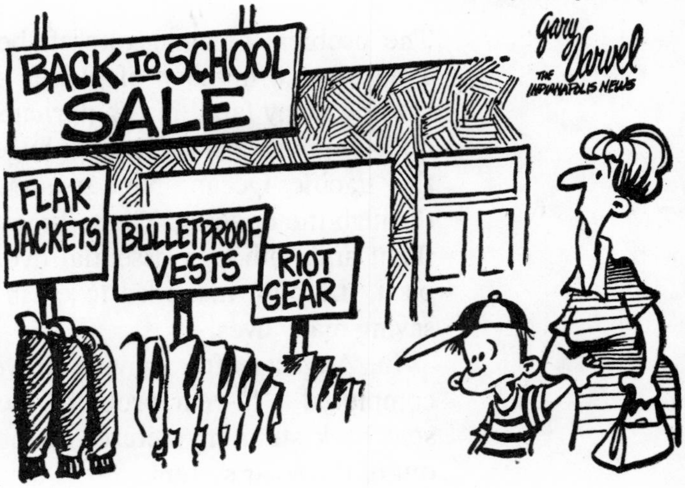

Gary Varvel
THE INDIANAPOLIS NEWS
BACK TO SCHOOL SALE
FLAK JACKETS
BULLETPROOF VESTS
RIOT GEAR

DAVID O'KEEFE
Courtesy Tampa Tribune

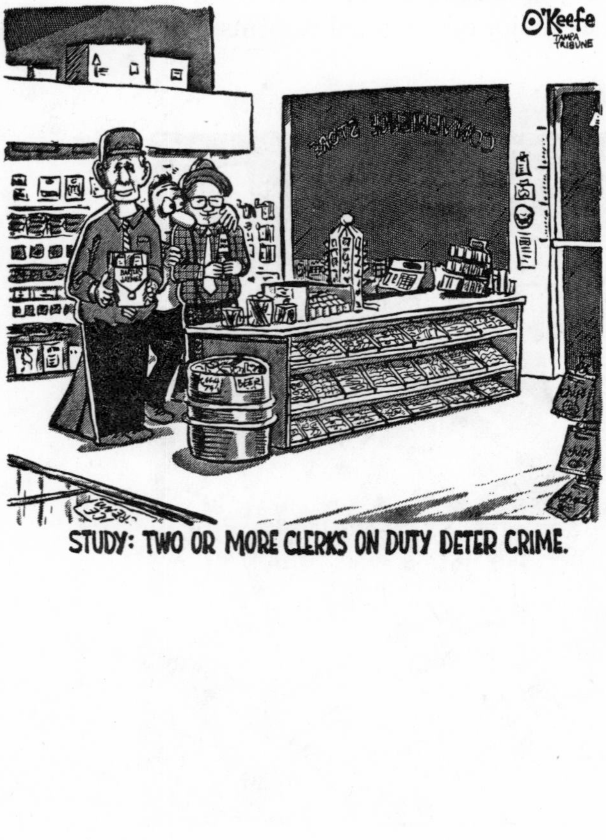

O'Keefe
TAMPA TRIBUNE
STUDY: TWO OR MORE CLERKS ON DUTY DETER CRIME.

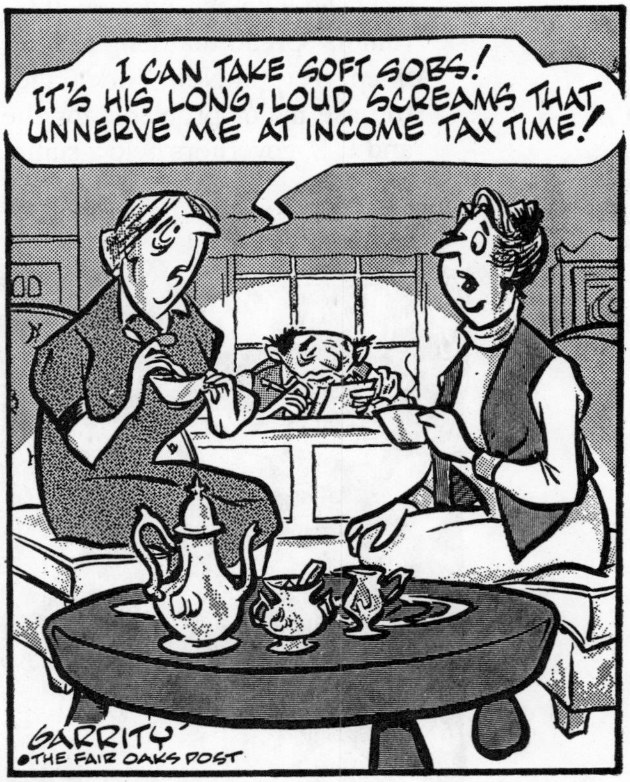

I CAN TAKE SOFT SOBS! IT'S HIS LONG, LOUD SCREAMS THAT UNNERVE ME AT INCOME TAX TIME!
GARRITY
©THE FAIR OAKS POST

MARTIN GARRITY
Courtesy Fair Oaks Post (Calif.)

BOB GORRELL
Courtesy Richmond News-Leader

"WE HAVE *ANOTHER* PROBLEM. . . . SHE WANTS THEIR FROZEN EMBRYOS, BUT HE WANTS THEIR REFRIGERATOR/FREEZER! . . ."

JIMMY MARGULIES
Courtesy Houston Post

JOHN KNUDSEN
Courtesy The Tidings (Calif.)

CLAY BENNETT
Courtesy St. Petersburg Times

LARRY WRIGHT
Courtesy Detroit News

ED FISCHER
Courtesy Rochester Post-Bulletin

CHRIS CURTIS
Courtesy Alexandria Gazette-Packet

HALF TIME AT NEW YORK GIANTS FOOTBALL STADIUM

DAVE GRANLUND
Courtesy Middlesex News

PETER WALLACE
Courtesy Boston Herald

WITH SLIMMER AIRLINE PROFITS, WHO FELT THE CUTBACKS MORE?
[A.] Airline executives [B.] Stockholders [C.] The passengers

TOM DARCY
Courtesy Newsday

SCOTT STANTIS
Courtesy Commercial Appeal

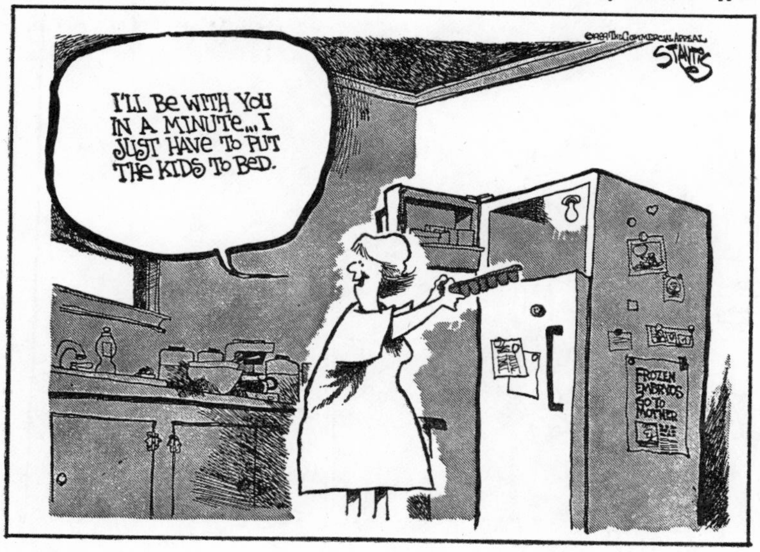

STANTIS
I'LL BE WITH YOU IN A MINUTE... I JUST HAVE TO PUT THE KIDS TO BED.
FROZEN EMBRYOS GO TO MOTHER

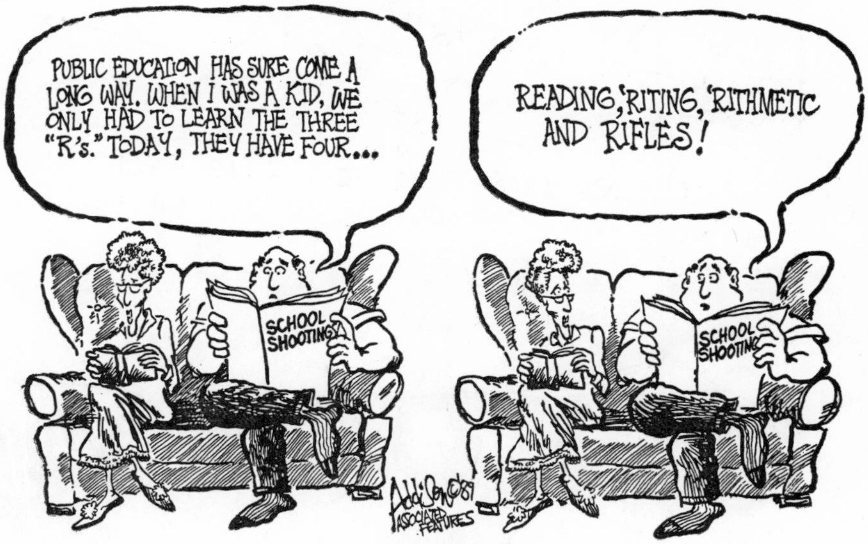

PUBLIC EDUCATION HAS SURE COME A LONG WAY. WHEN I WAS A KID, WE ONLY HAD TO LEARN THE THREE "R's." TODAY, THEY HAVE FOUR...
READING, 'RITING, 'RITHMETIC AND RIFLES!
SCHOOL SHOOTINGS
SCHOOL SHOOTINGS
Addison '89
ASSOCIATED FEATURES

TOM ADDISON
Courtesy Associated Features

DAVID HORSEY
Courtesy Seattle Post-Intelligencer

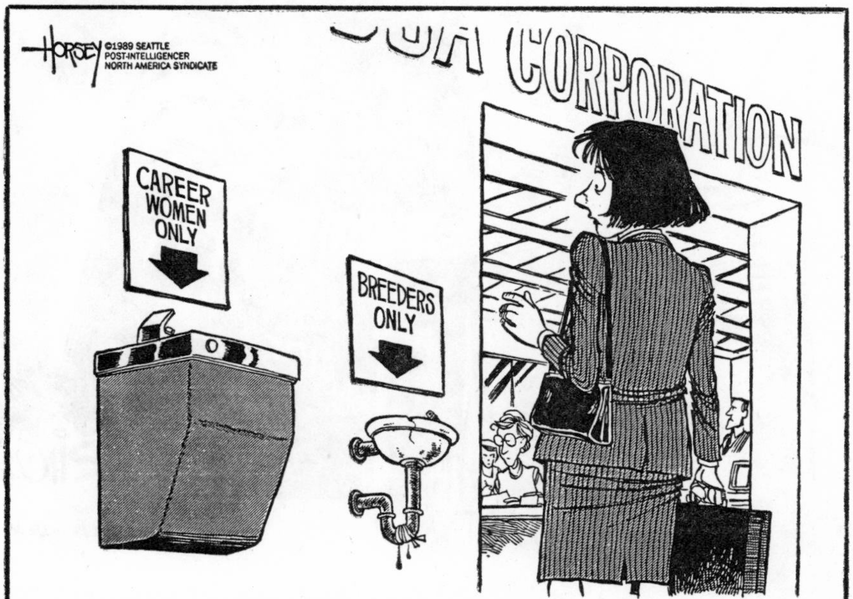

HORSEY
©1989 SEATTLE POST-INTELLIGENCER NORTH AMERICA SYNDICATE
CORPORATION
CAREER WOMEN ONLY
BREEDERS ONLY

WAYNE STAYSKAL
Courtesy Tampa Tribune

"I SAY IT'S TIME TO BRING BACK THE GOOD OLD DAYS OF STARVING ARTISTS!"

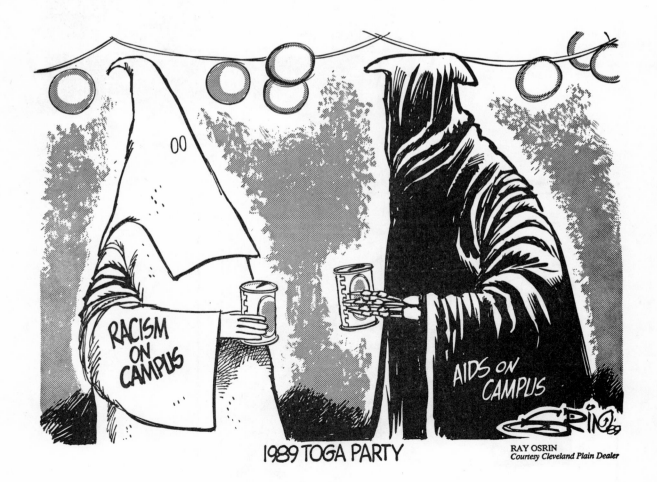

1989 TOGA PARTY

RAY OSRIN
Courtesy Cleveland Plain Dealer

TOM GIBB
Courtesy Altoona Mirror

KIRK ANDERSON
Courtesy Madison Capital Times

PAUL FELL
Courtesy Lincoln Journal

HANK MCCLURE
Courtesy Lawton Constitution

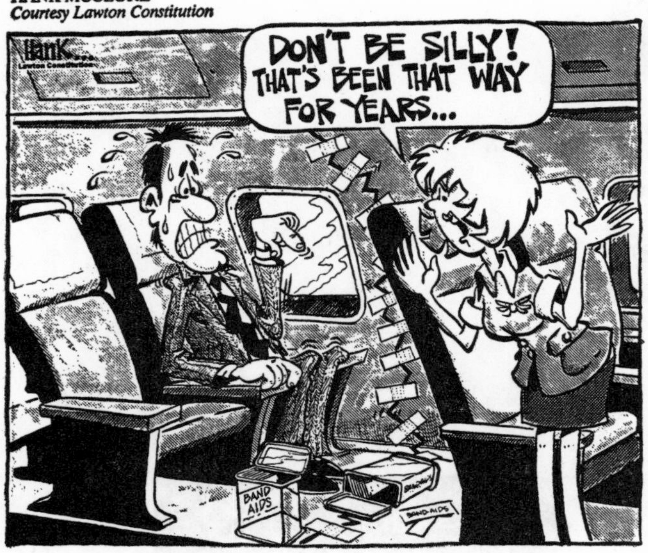

DON'T BE SILLY! THAT'S BEEN THAT WAY FOR YEARS...
BAND AIDS

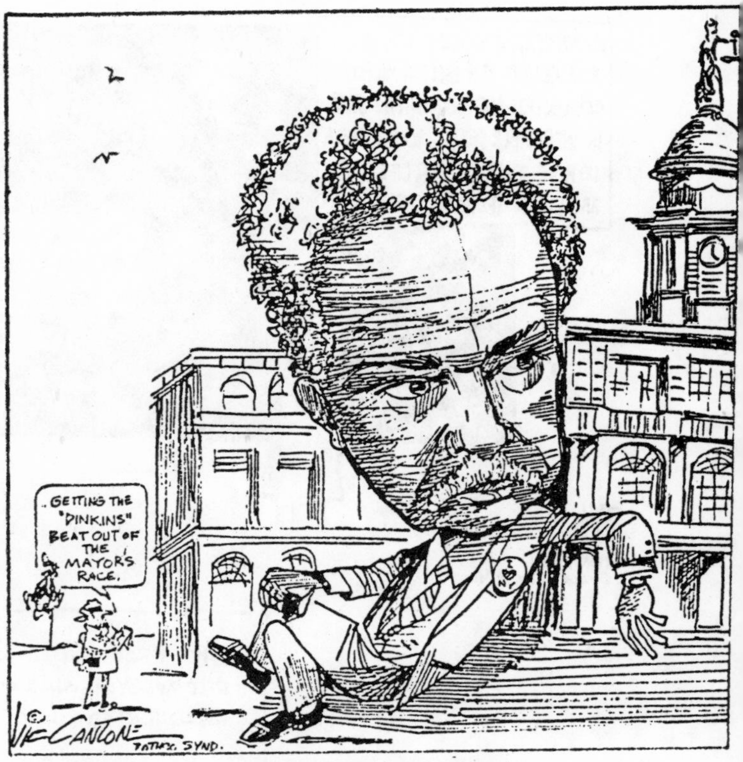

GETTING THE "DINKINS" BEAT OUT OF THE MAYOR'S RACE.
VIC CANTONE

VIC CANTONE
Courtesy Rothco

AUTUMN IN NEW YORK

BOB JORGENSEN
Courtesy Extra Newspaper Features

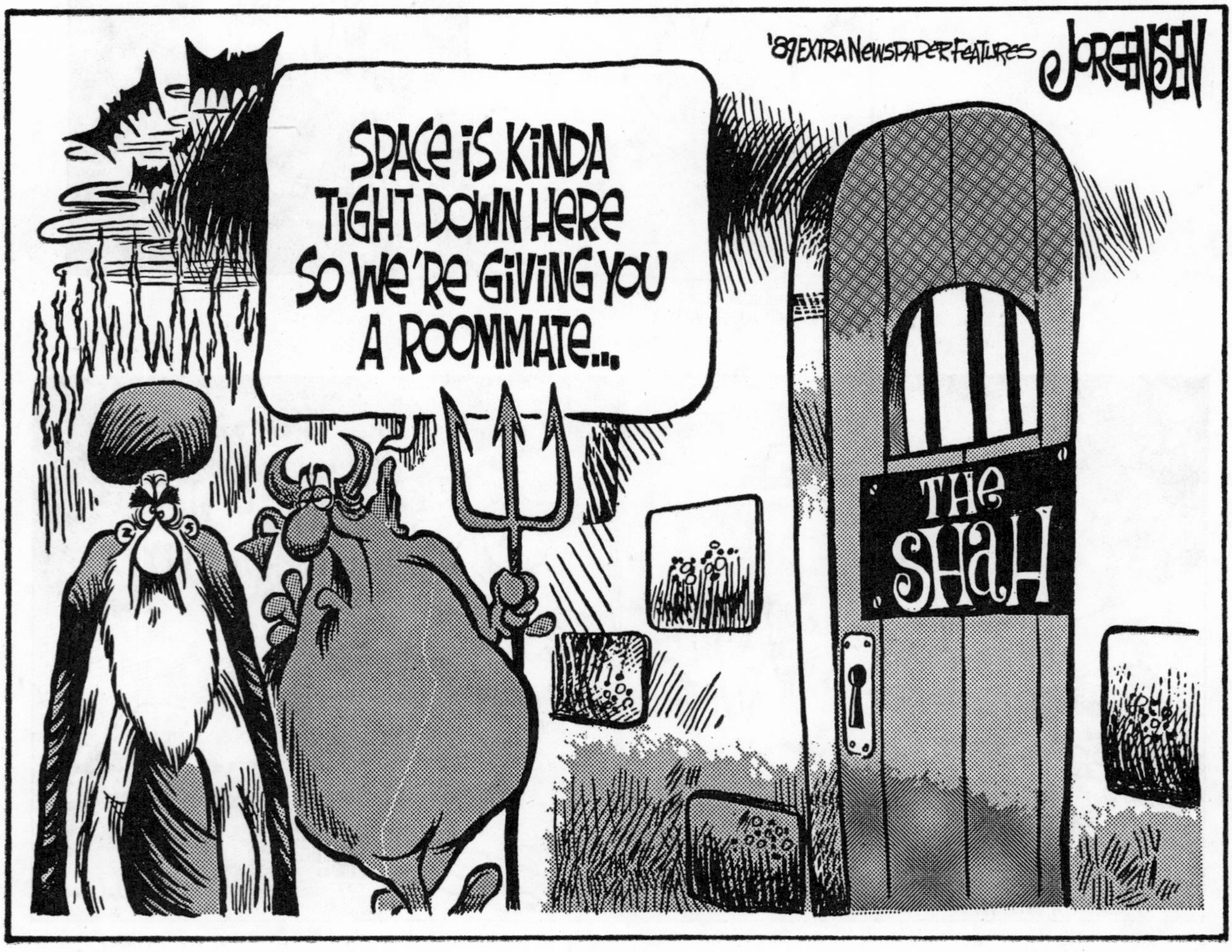

'89 EXTRA Newspaper Features JORGENSEN
SPACE IS KINDA TIGHT DOWN HERE SO WE'RE GIVING YOU A ROOMMATE...
THE SHAH

ED FISCHER
Courtesy Rochester Post-Bulletin

JIM DOBBINS
Courtesy Union Leader (N.H.)

BRUCE PLANTE
Courtesy Chattanooga Times

STEVE SACK
Courtesy Minneapolis Star-Tribune

Past Award Winners

NATIONAL SOCIETY OF PROFESSIONAL JOURNALISTS AWARD
(Formerly Sigma Delta Chi Award)

1942 – Jacob Burck, Chicago Times
1943 – Charles Werner, Chicago Sun
1944 – Henry Barrow, Associated Press
1945 – Reuben L. Goldberg, New York Sun
1946 – Dorman H. Smith, NEA
1947 – Bruce Russell, Los Angeles Times
1948 – Herbert Block, Washington Post
1949 – Herbert Block, Washington Post
1950 – Bruce Russell, Los Angeles Times
1951 – Herbert Block, Washington Post, and
        Bruce Russell, Los Angeles Times
1952 – Cecil Jensen, Chicago Daily News
1953 – John Fischetti, NEA
1954 – Calvin Alley, Memphis Commercial Appeal
1955 – John Fischetti, NEA
1956 – Herbert Block, Washington Post
1957 – Scott Long, Minneapolis Tribune
1958 – Clifford H. Baldowski, Atlanta Constitution
1959 – Charles G. Brooks, Birmingham News
1960 – Dan Dowling, New York Herald-Tribune
1961 – Frank Interlandi, Des Moines Register
1962 – Paul Conrad, Denver Post
1963 – William Mauldin, Chicago Sun-Times
1964 – Charles Bissell, Nashville Tennessean
1965 – Roy Justus, Minneapolis Star
1966 – Patrick Oliphant, Denver Post
1967 – Eugene Payne, Charlotte Observer
1968 – Paul Conrad, Los Angeles Times
1969 – William Mauldin, Chicago Sun-Times
1970 – Paul Conrad, Los Angeles Times
1971 – Hugh Haynie, Louisville Courier-Journal
1972 – William Mauldin, Chicago Sun-Times
1973 – Paul Szep, Boston Globe
1974 – Mike Peters, Dayton Daily News
1975 – Tony Auth, Philadelphia Enquirer
1976 – Paul Szep, Boston Globe
1977 – Don Wright, Miami News
1978 – Jim Borgman, Cincinnati Enquirer
1979 – John P. Trever, Albuquerque Journal
1980 – Paul Conrad, Los Angeles Times
1981 – Paul Conrad, Los Angeles Times
1982 – Dick Locher, Chicago Tribune
1983 – Rob Lawlor, Philadelphia Daily News
1984 – Mike Lane, Baltimore Evening Sun
1985 – Doug Marlette, Charlotte Observer
1986 – Mike Keefe, Denver Post
1987 – Paul Conrad, Los Angeles Times
1988 – Jack Higgins, Chicago Sun-Times

NATIONAL HEADLINERS CLUB AWARD

1938 – C. D. Batchelor, New York Daily News
1939 – John Knott, Dallas News
1940 – Herbert Block, NEA
1941 – Charles H. Sykes, Philadelphia Evening Ledger
1942 – Jerry Doyle, Philadelphia Record
1943 – Vaughn Shoemaker, Chicago Daily News
1944 – Roy Justus, Sioux City Journal
1945 – F. O. Alexander, Philadelphia Bulletin
1946 – Hank Barrow, Associated Press
1947 – Cy Hungerford, Pittsburgh Post-Gazette
1948 – Tom Little, Nashville Tennessean
1949 – Bruce Russell, Los Angeles Times
1950 – Dorman Smith, NEA
1951 – C. G. Werner, Indianapolis Star
1952 – John Fischetti, NEA
1953 – James T. Berryman and
        Gib Crocket, Washington Star
1954 – Scott Long, Minneapolis Tribune
1955 – Leo Thiele, Los Angeles Mirror-News
1956 – John Milt Morris, Associated Press
1957 – Frank Miller, Des Moines Register
1958 – Burris Jenkins, Jr., New York Journal-American
1959 – Karl Hubenthal, Los Angeles Examiner
1960 – Don Hesse, St. Louis Globe-Democrat
1961 – L. D. Warren, Cincinnati Enquirer
1962 – Franklin Morse, Los Angeles Mirror
1963 – Charles Bissell, Nashville Tennessean
1964 – Lou Grant, Oakland Tribune
1965 – Merle R. Tingley, London (Ont.) Free Press
1966 – Hugh Haynie, Louisville Courier-Journal
1967 – Jim Berry, NEA
1968 – Warren King, New York News
1969 – Larry Barton, Toledo Blade
1970 – Bill Crawford, NEA
1971 – Ray Osrin, Cleveland Plain Dealer
1972 – Jacob Burck, Chicago Sun-Times
1973 – Ranan Lurie, New York Times
1974 – Tom Darcy, Newsday
1975 – Bill Sanders, Milwaukee Journal
1976 – No award given
1977 – Paul Szep, Boston Globe
1978 – Dwane Powell, Raleigh News and Observer
1979 – Pat Oliphant, Washington Star
1980 – Don Wright, Miami News
1981 – Bill Garner, Memphis Commercial Appeal
1982 – Mike Peters, Dayton Daily News
1983 – Doug Marlette, Charlotte Observer
1984 – Steve Benson, Arizona Republic
1985 – Bill Day, Detroit Free Press
1986 – Mike Keefe, Denver Post
1987 – Mike Peters, Dayton Daily News
1988 – Doug Marlette, Charlotte Observer
1989 – Walt Handelsman, Scranton Times

PULITZER PRIZE

1922 – Rollin Kirby, New York World
1923 – No award given
1924 – J. N. Darling, New York Herald Tribune
1925 – Rollin Kirby, New York World
1926 – D. R. Fitzpatrick, St. Louis Post-Dispatch
1927 – Nelson Harding, Brooklyn Eagle
1928 – Nelson Harding, Brooklyn Eagle
1929 – Rollin Kirby, New York World
1930 – Charles Macauley, Brooklyn Eagle
1931 – Edmund Duffy, Baltimore Sun
1932 – John T. McCutcheon, Chicago Tribune
1933 – H. M. Talburt, Washington Daily News
1934 – Edmund Duffy, Baltimore Sun
1935 – Ross A. Lewis, Milwaukee Journal
1936 – No award given
1937 – C. D. Batchelor, New York Daily News
1938 – Vaughn Shoemaker, Chicago Daily News
1939 – Charles G. Werner, Daily Oklahoman
1940 – Edmund Duffy, Baltimore Sun
1941 – Jacob Burck, Chicago Times
1942 – Herbert L. Block, NEA
1943 – Jay N. Darling, New York Herald Tribune
1944 – Clifford K. Berryman, Washington Star
1945 – Bill Mauldin, United Features Syndicate
1946 – Bruce Russell, Los Angeles Times
1947 – Vaughn Shoemaker, Chicago Daily News
1948 – Reuben L. ("Rube") Goldberg, New York Sun
1949 – Lute Pease, Newark Evening News
1950 – James T. Berryman, Washington Star
1951 – Reginald W. Manning, Arizona Republic
1952 – Fred L. Packer, New York Mirror
1953 – Edward D. Kuekes, Cleveland Plain Dealer
1954 – Herbert L. Block, Washington Post
1955 – Daniel R. Fitzpatrick, St. Louis Post-Dispatch
1956 – Robert York, Louisville Times
1957 – Tom Little, Nashville Tennessean
1958 – Bruce M. Shanks, Buffalo Evening News
1959 – Bill Mauldin, St. Louis Post-Dispatch
1960 – No award given
1961 – Carey Orr, Chicago Tribune
1962 – Edmund S. Valtman, Hartford Times
1963 – Frank Miller, Des Moines Register
1964 – Paul Conrad, Denver Post
1965 – No award given
1966 – Don Wright, Miami News
1967 – Patrick B. Oliphant, Denver Post
1968 – Eugene Gray Payne, Charlotte Observer
1969 – John Fischetti, Chicago Daily News
1970 – Thomas F. Darcy, Newsday
1971 – Paul Conrad, Los Angeles Times
1972 – Jeffrey K. MacNelly, Richmond News Leader
1973 – No award given
1974 – Paul Szep, Boston Globe
1975 – Garry Trudeau, Universal Press Syndicate
1976 – Tony Auth, Philadelphia Enquirer
1977 – Paul Szep, Boston Globe
1978 – Jeff MacNelly, Richmond News Leader
1979 – Herbert Block, Washington Post
1980 – Don Wright, Miami News
1981 – Mike Peters, Dayton Daily News
1982 – Ben Sargent, Austin American-Statesman
1983 – Dick Locher, Chicago Tribune
1984 – Paul Conrad, Los Angeles Times
1985 – Jeff MacNelly, Chicago Tribune
1986 – Jules Feiffer, Universal Press Syndicate
1987 – Berke Breathed, Washington Post Writers Group
1988 – Doug Marlette, Atlanta Constitution
1989 – Jack Higgins, Chicago Sun-Times

NATIONAL NEWSPAPER AWARD / CANADA

1949 – Jack Boothe, Toronto Globe and Mail
1950 – James G. Reidford, Montreal Star
1951 – Len Norris, Vancouver Sun
1952 – Robert La Palme, Le Devoir, Montreal
1953 – Robert W. Chambers, Halifax Chronicle-Herald
1954 – John Collins, Montreal Gazette
1955 – Merle R. Tingley, London Free Press
1956 – James G. Reidford, Toronto Globe and Mail
1957 – James G. Reidford, Toronto Globe and Mail
1958 – Raoul Hunter, Le Soleil, Quebec
1959 – Duncan Macpherson, Toronto Star
1960 – Duncan Macpherson, Toronto Star
1961 – Ed McNally, Montreal Star
1962 – Duncan Macpherson, Toronto Star
1963 – Jan Kamienski, Winnipeg Tribune
1964 – Ed McNally, Montreal Star
1965 – Duncan Macpherson, Toronto Star
1966 – Robert W. Chambers, Halifax Chronicle-Herald
1967 – Raoul Hunter, Le Soleil, Quebec
1968 – Roy Peterson, Vancouver Sun
1969 – Edward Uluschak, Edmonton Journal
1970 – Duncan Macpherson, Toronto Daily Star
1971 – Yardley Jones, Toronto Star
1972 – Duncan Macpherson, Toronto Star
1973 – John Collins, Montreal Gazette
1974 – Blaine, Hamilton Spectator
1975 – Roy Peterson, Vancouver Sun
1976 – Andy Donato, Toronto Sun
1977 – Terry Mosher, Montreal Gazette
1978 – Terry Mosher, Montreal Gazette
1979 – Edd Uluschak, Edmonton Journal
1980 – Vic Roschkov, Toronto Star
1981 – Tom Innes, Calgary Herald
1982 – Blaine, Hamilton Spectator
1983 – Dale Cummings, Winnipeg Free Press
1984 – Roy Peterson, Vancouver Sun
1985 – Ed Franklin, Toronto Globe and Mail
1986 – Brian Gable, Regina Leader Post
1987 – Raffi Anderian, Ottawa Citizen
1988 – Vance Rodewalt, Calgary Herald

Index

INDEX